Kenneth Wydro has conducted effective speaking seminars for numerous major corporations, including General Foods, Avon Products, and E.F. Hutton. He is the author of two previous books and is a frequent speaker at national conventions and conferences.

THINK ON YOUR FEET

The Art of Thinking and Speaking Under Pressure

KENNETH WYDRO

A FIRESIDE BOOK
Published by Simon & Schuster
New York London Toronto Sydney Tokyo Singapore

Simon & Schuster Building
Rockefeller Center
1230 Avenue of the Americas
New York, New York 10020

Library of Congress Cataloging in Publication Data
WYDRO, KENNETH
    Think on your feet.

    1.   Interpersonal communication.   2.   Public
speaking.   3.   Thought and thinking.   4.   Stress
(Psychology)   5.   Success.   I.   Title.
HM132.W92   808.5'01'9   80-27392
ISBN: 0-671-76538-8

To Vy Higginsen,

*Partner in need,
     in seed,
     in deed*

Contents

Preface

An unforgettable experience in human life is the moment of discovery of a great universal truth. That flash of insight — the sensation when the light of inner understanding goes on — can shape and direct the discoverer into an entirely new quality and meaning of life.

Although there are certain laws and principles that operate all the time, twenty-four hours a day, we have to discover them for ourselves if they are to have any practical meaning. Long before Thomas Edison lived, the principles of electricity existed. He discovered how to channel and focus the natural laws into practical means. He gave the world a special kind of light that altered the quality of contemporary living.

Great thinkers throughout history have told us that a genius is not a person who has been granted special talents or powers, but is one who has focused and specialized that natural talent or power. Each one of us is a potential genius with a private pipeline into a creative reservoir that is as available as electricity. Everything depends on what we do with what we have.

The major thought at the foundation of this book is not original, but is one I came to discover for myself much as Edison discovered how to use electricity — through long years of experiment and practice, in my case in the field of human relationships. The thought was first clearly articulated for me by Eric Butterworth of the Unity Center in New York City, who pointed to Ralph Waldo Emerson's essay, *Circles*.

The basic concept that helped transform my life of thought and professional expertise was simple and direct.

Around every circle, a larger circle may be drawn.

Around every set of experiences, a larger set of experiences may evolve. No matter the mistakes and limitations of the past, a more fulfilling and prosperous life can be sculpted. Around every fence or boundary, there is an open field ready to be cultivated and harvested. Around every circle, a larger circle may be drawn.

Edison conducted his experiments in a scientific laboratory; I researched the findings of this book as an instructor in several branches of the City University of New York, in professional theatre study with Lee Strasberg and David LeGrant, in the training seminar rooms of many large corporations in America, and in many courses with leaders of the New Thought Movement, most notably Dr. Butterworth in New York. Years of investigation in the art of communications have revealed a startling psychological fact. *Within us is the cause of what happens to us.* We are very much like living magnets, attracting the kind and quality of experience that we are thinking and feeling about in the private domain of our own minds. Our fears, worries, and concerns come true first. More important than what is happening to us or around us is what is happening *in* us.

Nowhere is this principle more apparent than in an effective presentations seminar. When asked to stand up and say a few words in front of a group of peers, thousands of people have revealed that their inner world is the cause of their outer experience. Their personal fears or inhibitions actually caused limitations and pressures in their everyday lives. Yet, because the fears and limitations were essentially an unconscious choice born out of a lack of consciousness and awareness of their true strength and potential, it was possible to change ingrained patterns by helping them *understand* that they could control their thoughts, feelings, and desires anytime they really wanted to.

Essentially, people give up their power and right to a happy, creative, and prosperous life because of poor training and a strong addiction to external stimulations from the world "out there." Although formal education may teach us about history, physical science, and mathematics, it rarely teaches us about ourselves and our deepest potentials. Many of us have left our lives up to chance and the set of circumstances around us. But when we take our own training into our own hands, we come to see that we are responsible for ourselves and what happens to us. Nobody is doing *it* to us. We author our own books, whether we know it or not.

The purpose of *Think on Your Feet* is to stimulate you toward the consciousness that you *are* your own boss. No matter your work or profession, you need to be in the *express* business — the business of expressing yourself and articulating your own personal, unique, individual talent. As you think clearer and speak with greater poise and confidence, you will find yourself expanding into larger and larger circles.

As more and more doctors and psychologists are revealing to us every year, the greatest enemy of healthy, happy living and excellent expression of our inner selves is worry, strain, pressure. The body, for example, is biased toward health. If you break a bone, the natural healing forces will begin to set it right. You do not have to do anything to start those forces in motion — they are there already, built into the human system.

The point is that there are also laws and *principles of communication* that work all the time. We have to unlearn some errors and see those laws and principles clearly. We have to cooperate with them to benefit and gain the rewards. We have to wire our own houses and flick the switches to use the electrical forces. That is why I draw a larger circle around the traditional method of teaching effective speaking and thinking techniques.

This is a wholistic approach. The anxiety, nervous manner-isms, and unconscious glaze that come over many people when they are asked to speak spontaneously or express a deep emotion are merely symptoms of a deeper and more significant state of mind. The boil can be treated physically, but something else is happening psychologically. The boil is the effect, not the cause, which runs much deeper than the external symptom.

In the past, teaching "public speaking" or effective speak-ing has treated the effect and the symptom, but not the cause. We have been giving students of all levels "emergency treatment," put-ting bandaids on sores when we could just as easily treat and focus in on the *cause* level of consciousness. Very simply, when people really catch the idea that they have control over their bodies, feelings and thoughts, a magnificent and wonderful transformation occurs. Many, many times in the *Think on Your Feet* seminar that I conduct in many cities in the United States, I have witnessed a shy, timid, re-pressed person come out of a shell and experience a new light on life. More times, I have seen a competent, functioning, talented profes-sional raise his or her game one notch higher and gain the "slight edge" on competition. Over and over again, participants of the seminar have reported that they were producing more and better under pressure. The very situations that used to leave them frus-trated, uptight, and numb were now the opportunities to advance and make favorable impressions.

In a short period of time, it is possible to shed layers and layers of dead emotional skin and come into yourself in a new and thrilling way. You *can* draw a larger circle around the same situations that used to ruffle your feathers and push your hot button. You can create your own opportunity to fly higher, with your tank filled up with a super, high test fuel.

You can develop confidence, poise, and style in many dif-ferent ways, but this book offers you a way that is *joyous, creative,* and *imaginative.* The exercises in this book *work* — but they work differently for everyone. The electricity is there, but we choose the kind of bulb and lamp to channel the force. I urge and encourage you to read these chapters and try these exercises in a playful spirit. Nothing here is to be practiced with a sense of a final examination or job appraisal review coming up. Play with them without the pressure of having to do them "right" or "well". The more you enjoy the pro-cess of growth, the more these exercises will reveal yourself to yourself. The chances are unbeatable that you will like what you find.

Everything in this book might not speak to your personal needs and desires, but you will definitely find something you can use. Something in this book will light a light or spark a feeling. If you can get one piece of news you can use, you can change the quality of your present circle. Take the best, leave the rest.

The success of any idea, product, or service depends on your ability to communicate effectively. Around every circle, a larger circle may be drawn. To your success!

1

All Those Eyes

Have you ever been called on to speak before a group of people unexpectedly?

Have you ever found yourself in an emotional confrontation with a boss, a family member, or a stranger and felt a complete loss of words?

Have you ever walked away from a meeting or interaction with another person thinking of what you should have said — five minutes after the incident was over?

How do you react to situations where you must "think on your feet"? How do you respond to deadlines, to pressures, to demands upon you from the outside world?

1

When you find yourself in the center of controversy, how well do you stand up to "all those eyes"?

All those eyes is a psychological reaction that can come over you whenever you have to stand before an audience or deal with an emotional person in your everyday environment. It is the sudden, often paralyzing sensation that people out there are looking at you, seeing through you, staring into you, judging you harshly, condemning you, making fun of you, laughing at you behind your back, cutting you to shreds. It doesn't matter if you are a top business executive, a budding actor or actress, a parent who is addressing the local P.T.A., or a lover having an emotional argument with your latest flame. Somehow, when you are standing alone, in front of other people, (or even going one-on-one in a heated situation) "all those eyes" out there can be a terrifying, threatening, and intimidating factor, which reduces you to less than what you really are. No matter how intelligent you are or how long you have prepared for a presentation or final examination, there is always the split second when you will have to confront, engage, and overcome "all those eyes."

A high-ranking corporate executive once reported, "I was perfectly composed at the beginning, before I took the platform. I was confident. I was prepared — until I saw all those eyes. Then the lights went out. I went blank — embarrassed myself terribly. I'll never forget the deadly silence or that horrible feeling of helplessness. I was cold and sweating at the same time. My mouth was dry. It was a nightmare — something I never want to experience again." Another highly qualified business person identified the condition in another way. "As soon as I stand up, my mind sits down."

There is no doubt about it. Performing under pressure is a moment of truth. Whenever there is something at stake, you reveal yourself by how you speak, think, and act. Some people crumble under pressure and avoid revealing themselves at all costs. Others thrive under pressure, feeling that crisis is the perfect time to express what they think and how they feel.

This book has one major idea and purpose behind it: *to help you think better under pressure.* No matter what business, profession, or field you are in, you will perform better when you can speak with poise, confidence, and assurance. The person who can think on his or her feet and respond to the pressure in a positive way attracts opportunity — for personal, financial, and emotional growth. Those people who cannot think quickly under pressure often find themselves in holding patterns for years, victims of circumstance, caught in a system that seems to strangle their creativity and suppress their individuality.

It is very important to understand from the very beginning that thinking on your feet is not a capacity that some have and others do not. *Thinking on your feet is a mental habit.* You have — inside of you right now — the ability to think quickly and speak with confidence. Your job is to cultivate that capacity. You have a creative seed within you all the time. Everything depends on how you treat yourself, how you see yourself, what you believe about yourself.

Whenever you face an important deadline, an unresponsive colleague, or an emotionally inflamed partner, there is only one major idea to keep in mind — more important than what is happening *around* you or *to* you is what is happening *in* you. The pressure, the circumstances, the irritating people are all *outside* of you, but your reaction is *inside* of you. You can allow those people or things out there to push your buttons, or you can push your own buttons. You can let them determine your emotional temperature, or you can regulate your temperature from within. You can be a thermometer or a thermostat.

As you know, the thermometer simply registers the temperature of the environment around it. On a hot day, the red liquid goes up. On a cold day, it goes down. In this sense, the thermometer is a mere reporter of external conditions. In that sense, it is at the mercy of circumstances beyond its control. The thermostat, however, regulates the environmental temperature from within. It keeps the environment in check and balance. In this sense, the thermostat is the conductor and the arranger.

When asked to stand up and say a few words, or when dealing with some unresponsive, uncooperative person, do you regulate your emotions and thoughts from within? Or do you let the situation or the personality of the other person determine your emotional temperature?

The most effective, dynamic, confident speakers all demonstrate what might be called the *thermostat consciousness.* Whenever they feel the heat, cold, or pressure from the outside, they have something within themselves working for them. Instead of reacting to the outside, external conditions, they work, think, and speak *from the inside out.*

Those who can rise to the difficult occasion and thrive under pressure always have a level of mind working in them and for them. They tune into a wavelength or frequency of thought inside themselves, which then tends to regulate all the influences around them. This inner wavelength is their secret for success. No matter what is happening around or to them, the most important thing is what is happening in them.

The fundamental insight in dealing with "all those eyes" is that pressure and tension are something that happen inside of you *as a reaction* to what is happening on the outside of you. Since you always have the capacity to be a human thermostat and regulate your own temperature from within, you can use pressure, tension, disappointment, or delay as a cue to your own creativity. The external conditions — the economy, the budget crunch, the irritating personality of a co-worker — are not as significant as your reactions to them.

What is at stake here is your power of choice. When you allow the outer conditions to determine your inner state of mind, you give away your power. You reduce yourself by pushing your tense, anxious, frightened button. But it is important to understand from the very beginning of our study that *nobody is doing it to you!*

When you dry up or go blank in a crisis situation, you are not tuning into a potential within you that is present all the time. When you think of what you should have said five minutes after the encounter is over, you have made *a choice*, unconscious as it might be. The trick is to change your unconscious, blind, habitual reactions to conscious, deliberate, thoughtful actions. Instead of naively expecting the outside world to give you positive input, the creative, spontaneous effective communicator understands that he or she must flick on an inside switch when the going gets tough.

It's important to establish and practice *an inner control.* It's important to wire your own house with electricity if you want to have light in the dark. It's important to light up your mind — for in the mind there is the power to overcome the terrible anxiety, fear, and insecurity when facing the tough customer, the domineering boss, or the emotionally upset partner.

The first place you have to look if you truly want to

improve yourself in the art of interpersonal communications is inside yourself. You may have all the proper degrees, book knowledge, and technical expertise. But how do you speak to people? How do you express yourself when the heat is on? What do you call upon when you have to produce under pressure?

The first step is a clear understanding that you do not have to learn more formulas or techniques. You don't really have to take another class or acquire another degree to be able to think on your feet and say words that make a positive difference to people around you. You don't have to study the larynx or speech systems of the physical mechanism. You don't have to learn all about the formalities of proper enunciation or the intricacies of parliamentary procedure. But you do have to learn about your own innate, natural capacities and use what you already have. Thinking on your feet is more a matter of expressing what is already there than adding something new to your system.

What you have to do is learn to relax, concentrate, and prepare your inner self, which will help you deal effectively with everything that happens out there. Most of us have been trained to depend on the "out there" for our personal meaning, worth, and state of happiness, but a whole new direction takes shape when we learn to take time for ourselves — to invest thought, energy, and time in the development of our own natural resources.

In this light, the first stage of our creative process is to understand the primary roles of *relaxation, concentration,* and *preparation* in the entire creative process.

RELAXATION

Relaxation is the key to the vault of riches.

Have you ever noticed that when you are relaxed, at ease, in tune with yourself and the moment, ideas seem to come to you? Without even really trying, words will flow spontaneously and easily — mainly because you are not worrying whether they are right or wrong, good or bad, appropriate or inappropriate. Have you ever really stopped to notice that when you relax your defenses, dissolve your fears, and enjoy yourself, another level of your mind seems to operate?

When we say that relaxation is the key to the vault of riches, we mean that you have an entire storeroom of talent and creativity inside of yourself that is waiting to be opened, used, and cultivated. Very often, the *idea* of speaking before a group or articulating what we really feel sets off a chain reaction of fear, worry, and inferiority. Very often, the idea of thinking on your feet is much worse than the actual event.

Yet, for those who choose to relax and enjoy themselves, speaking in public and overcoming past limitations and poor habits become a tremendous victory and opportunity for success. You have to see and believe first in yourself — in that inner reservoir of intelligence, creativity, and feeling that makes you a unique individual.

It has always seemed to me that the genie in the Aladdin and the Lamp story did not really live in a magic lamp on the shelf of Aladdin's house, but actually dwelled within Aladdin himself. Once you get the idea that there is a "genie" inside of you, a tremendous, almost miraculous transformation takes place. There is a presence within yourself that can grant you "three wishes" and guide you to the right and proper action when you call upon that presence in the right way. You can summon up your secret powers, just like Aladdin, anytime you want when you remember to *relax under pressure.* Whenever something or someone out there bugs, frustrates, or irritates you, call upon that presence. *Relax.*

Relax what? Relax your body — your shoulders, your eyebrows, your back. Relax for just a moment before you respond. Before you speak, act, or react to that outside force, check your inner playing field. The truth of the matter is that you think better, feel better, speak better when you are controlling yourself from within.

It's a choice you make. It's an idea that you set in motion from within. It's your own personal genie that can get you through all tight, tense, anxious situations. If you don't know what to do or what to say, relax.

It's very refreshing to know, understand, and believe in this power of relaxation. And very comforting to know that under times of stress and strain that a deep breath, a loosening of the eyebrows, a lowering of the shoulders can have such a powerful impact on the entire psyche, and thus on the environmental conditions.

Time after time in seminars, training programs, and in-the-field experiences, the very command of "relax your shoulders" has given an entirely new perspective on the events and the circumstances of the moment. If you can remember to relax your shoulders, you will find that outside influences will lose their sting and their power over you. Once you consistently practice relaxing your shoulders under pressure, you will find that ideas begin to flow into you spontaneously, almost as if something inside has been waiting for this moment to express.

The problem, of course, is social conditioning. We have been taught that environmental conditions are stronger than the power of choice. As a society and culture, we have not been urged to relax under pressure. We have been told to "get a grasp on yourself," "have a stiff upper lip," or "hold on for dear life." We have been encouraged to blast down the door rather than find the key to open it easily and gracefully. We have been taught to suppress our emotions and reach out for security rather than reach in for power, poise, and pressure-proof activity.

Therefore, the first and most essential phase of learning to overcome the external pressures of the world is to focus on your ability to *choose* relaxation instead of resistance, resentment, or refutation. It really does not matter whether you are facing a job review, being interviewed for a new position, dealing with a stubborn child, or selling to an irritating client. When you mentally resist the outside stimulus, you wage war *against yourself*. No matter what is happening around you or to you, the most important thing is what is happening in you. The first turn toward success comes when you remind yourself to relax and find that center of calm within yourself that is always there, always present, always available.

The most interesting and most subtle aspect to this shift in consciousness is that the turning point invariably happens *in a situation of crisis*. You can expect the unexpected. As if by some master plan, you will be confronting a hostile, uncooperative client or colleague. You will come face to face with an unruly, unresponsive child. You will be in an enraged romantic tussle with a present or former emotional partner, and the heat will be on. Suddenly, out of somewhere, you will remember to relax your shoulders and raise your thinking one notch higher, and everything will change. You will help create crisis after crisis until you learn to shift your emotional gears from that outer orientation to an inner one. Once you come to yourself by making a choice even though the pressure is on, you will see everything around you in a different light.

From such a camera angle, pressure points can be seen as signals for imminent growth and advancement. The pressure buildup only means that growth is happening. Your power of choice and self-control is about to be exercised. If you lose sight of your inher-- ent ability to control the emotional temperature inside you, you will be pulled apart and pushed around by outside forces. You will feel a vague, persistent anxiety, a sense of impending loss or doom, because you are uprooted from the true center of power.

The fear and anxiety, the sense of being out of control or ineffective — all those eyes — stems mainly from lack of perspective. Whenever you feel you have something to prove or an outside standard to live up to, you will be feeling the stress and strain that leads to poor performance under pressure. Especially when it comes to effective interpersonal communications, the great need is to learn how to relax and see the external circumstances in a new and differ- ent way.

To help you start practicing the crucial ability to relax under pressure, here are two good "warm-up" exercises to improve your power of choice in your daily environment.

The Attitude Break

Do you take a coffee or cigarette break at certain times during the work day? Do you feel yourself reaching for a piece of candy or a valium when you are irritated or pressured by deadlines? When the going gets tough, what do you reach for?

The *attitude break* is time given to yourself to step back and gain some perspective on the current situation before doing battle blindly. Your attitude is like gas in your car. Your car may have a powerful engine, luxurious upholstery, and the latest mechani- cal equipment, but it is going nowhere without the fuel. Likewise, you may have a beautiful face and body, with all the right edu- cational background, with all the important connections, but with- out the proper attitude, you will be going nowhere. Without your attitude gauge on positive, you will become your own worst enemy, plagued with a life of increasing frustration, tension, and melancholy.

The important idea here is that relaxation is an *attitude*, a way of meeting outside conditions from the inside. Like thoughts, attitudes can be chosen consciously and conditioned through practice. Instead of having your moods and feelings randomly coming and going out of control, take *an attitude break* to fill up your emotional gas tank. Especially when you feel pressure and sense "all those eyes" boring into you, take a minute to quiet down and turn inside your own mind and play a little game for a moment.

Make believe that you are feeling pressure while sitting in a rowboat next to a dock. You are in the boat with the oars in your hand, and you see the person or thing causing the pressure out there on the dock. Then, slowly but surely, see yourself rowing away from the dock. In your own mind, stroke your way over the water and see the problem on the dock getting smaller and smaller. Row away from the problem until you are far out to sea and you can hardly see the dock anymore. See the person or thing on the dock bathed in a spot of light. Take a couple of deep breaths, then go back and face the problem.

As you dissolve the pressure point in your own mind, you will find that your attitude tank is automatically filled up with positive fuel. To do this, simply set mental relaxation as a goal for your attitude break. It has been said that we become what we think. If we think in pressured, constricted terms, we will find ourselves in pressurized, constricted circumstances.

So, in the midmorning, at lunchtime, at the three o'clock slump period, take a few minutes to refuel your attitude tank. You may not want to do the rowboat exercise all the time; the important thing is to relax, let go, and change your mind about what "they" are doing to you. Your mental tightness is essentially your own choice. Since you have that power built into your system as a potential, you have the power to choose how you prefer to meet the external world.

As you practice your attitude break, you will find that you have a clearer insight into the problems "out there." You will be better able to focus in on what needs to be done to resolve the problem rather than wasting time and energy in bitterness, resentment, and complaining about other people. If you give yourself a regular attitude break several times during the course of your normal day, you will be part of the solution instead of being part of the problem.

As you teach yourself to navigate the ups and downs, the

hidden curves of your road, you will be very surprised to discover the many opportunities that will come to meet you without even trying. The ability to relax under pressure and express your own intuitive point of view is money in the bank.

The Telephone Game

Probably for most people, the telephone is an important element in life. In business, social, or personal affairs, the telephone often is the emotional focus. Whenever your phone rings, someone is trying to reach you. Whenever you pick it up, you are trying to communicate something to another human being.

A good way to practice relaxation and working from the inside out is to use the telephone as a signal to yourself. Whenever your phone rings, use the sound as a reminder first to relax your shoulders and your eyebrows. *Before you answer the phone, relax.* Deliberately set your attitude as one of positivity and relaxation. You do not know for certain who the caller is, so make it a game to meet the unexpected with your body and your mind relaxed.

The ringing phone, so often a nuisance and a distraction, can also be the cue for you to rise above it. The ringing phone can be a reminder for you to practice certain principles of effective communication. Before you pick it up, check yourself from the inside. Meet the unexpected with a specific attitude and frame of mind, as if every phone call you receive is an opportunity for positive exchange.

Meet the outside with an inner point of view and make the whole activity a game. In the beginning, you will probably have to deliberately remind yourself of your intention. But with practice, you will develop an ability to meet the unexpected with calm, poise, and assurance.

As with anything that approaches you from the outside, the telephone can be a tremendous ally when you respond to it with an inner state of relaxation. Whenever the phone rings, *relax*. Take a deep breath. Take a long look at it, then sit back. Take a brief moment for yourself before you go into action.

Take the telephone as a cue for you to meet that voice with your best self — your clear mind and your relaxed body. When you keep relaxed and open, you will find the right thing to say.

CONCENTRATION

If you ask any successful sports figure, artist, or business person the key to consistent, top performance, you will invariably hear the word *concentration* somewhere in the answer. The ability to concentrate, or focus, on a specific goal is an essential ingredient in any attempt to communicate effectively. Without a high level of concentration, words and actions randomly fly in and zoom out. Without concentration, communication lacks purpose and direction.

How well do you concentrate?

Do you find yourself with one major, directive purpose during the day, or are you split up and going in several different directions at one time? Do you believe that some people can concentrate naturally, and some can't? Are you someone who was left out when they passed around the ability to concentrate? What is your basic belief about yourself in the area of concentration?

Every person has the potential and natural ability to concentrate, but few set about exercising and developing this power in a regular way. It is important to see that the mental powers of concentration are very much like the muscles of the physical body. Certain habits can develop and strengthen the physical body, just as lazy habits or lack of care can weaken the body and make it vulnerable to disease.

For example, are you a worrier? A complainer? A pessimist? Have you felt consistent anger or animosity toward your job, your parents, your children, your neighbor? If you have, you have practiced concentration, although the critical mind has used the powers of concentration in a negative way.

If you tend to see the negative side of the situation at hand, you are setting yourself up for pressure. The worried or critical mind will always feel attacked when facing all those eyes. Because worriers always look for what can go wrong, they will see those aspects when under pressure. In effect, they will be their own worst enemies because they will cast themselves in adversary roles when dealing with others.

Concentration, then, is the focusing of what is already there inside of you. When you hold a magnifying glass over paper, you can focus the rays of the sun in such a way that you can light the paper on fire. No external power is really added. The same rays that warm the air burn the paper. The difference is in the concentration of the power that is already there. Likewise, if you can think at all, you can concentrate and raise your thinking one level higher.

The key to positive concentration powers is not to try to force yourself to concentrate. Instead of *making* yourself concentrate, *let* yourself concentrate. Perhaps the most effective way to concentrate is through the process of visualizations. A *visualization* is simply the mental picture you have in the back of your mind about yourself. For example, if your mental picture about yourself is one of holding back or holding in when facing your boss, your spouse, or some "crazy" person out there, your behavior will follow suit. Whatever you are picturing in your mind will play itself out in your actions in the field.

This is the phenomenon of the *self-fulfilling prophecy.* What many of us fail to realize is that everything we do is a self-fulfilling prophecy. If we can't see ourselves speaking before a group of people comfortably and easily, for example, we won't. If we can't see ourselves making a 20-percent increase in salary next year, we won't. If you see yourself leveled off in a certain job or industry, you will level off your performance.

The great trap is that it's so easy to picture, think about, and concentrate *on what we don't want to happen.* We often think about all the things that could go wrong. We wake up, get the news, shake our heads, and let the situations in the world give us our mental picture for the day. For example:

> *"How are you feeling today, Joe?"*
>
> *"I don't know. I'll tell you after I see what kind of mood my boss is in."*
>
> *"Well, what do you expect?"*
>
> *"More of the same crap,"* Joe often says, *without a spark of hope.*

The great insight in this entire matter of concentration is that *circumstances and events do not cause thoughts.* Events and circumstances are external — independent activities of your own mental field. Your thoughts are in you. Just as you choose certain clothes to wear for the day, you can also choose your thoughts or your moods.

People who have difficulty concentrating often work *from the outside in*. They wrap themselves in the "thermometer consciousness" every day, then complain, moan, and groan when they find themselves the victims of circumstances. When you wait for your boss to determine your mood for the day, you diminish your power of concentration. You let another person choose your thought or your mood *for* you. In effect, you cut yourself off from your talent and your capacity to rise above the external pressure when you look to the outside for meaning, support, or encouragement.

Of course, it is helpful to find yourself in a support system where you are wanted, liked, and appreciated. But you cannot depend on that for your own state of mind. If you truly desire to stand up to "all those eyes" and express the best within yourself, you have to unlearn your habit of letting others push your emotional buttons. In fact, the great trick in learning how to concentrate and speak effectively under pressure is to *unlearn* your old habits. Kick your environmental addictions. Let go of all the past events that tend to limit your ability to deal with the current moment.

Easier said than done, to be sure. But it is in this inner field, the inner space of your own mind, feelings, and desires that concentration really takes place. There is no way to get around the inner work on yourself. If you genuinely desire to get better, make more money, have greater freedom, express your unique talent, you must first turn within and begin to deal with your own thoughts and feelings about yourself.

This is not an easy thing for most people to do since we have been taught to look toward and depend upon the outside world for our satisfaction and meaning. But you can reverse that flow. You can change the circumstances of your life by altering your thoughts about those circumstances. You can picture what you want to happen rather than what you don't want to happen.

In order to tap your creative potential, which is always inside of you, begin to give yourself positive mental pictures. See what you want in completed form. See yourself making the sale, relaxing under pressure, laughing with your "enemy." See what you prefer to happen, as if it is *already done.*

Although there will be many exercises in concentration in later stages of this book to help you focus your powers and refine your natural ability to concentrate, there is a vital, major, important idea to catch here at the beginning. *Concentration is the focusing and harnessing of your inner thoughts.* No thought is more powerful than a visual picture.

In this whole matter of concentration, there is one bow to wrap up the entire package. We often have trouble concentrating, not because we know too little or have too few ambitions, but because we have so many. We know too much about the past that only intrudes upon the present. We let our failures and frustrations take root. We come to expect too little of ourselves.

The first phase of the remedy for this chronic problem is to *take time to slow down, to quiet, to relax, and to clear the mind.* Airplanes cannot land on crowded runways. Ideas cannot land on a cluttered mind. New clothes cannot be put into an already packed closet. You cannot concentrate when you *try* to concentrate.

The basic, fundamental principle brings the matter of concentration back down to you and what you feed your mind for breakfast. In the morning, it is very important to clear your mind, quiet your fears and frustrations, *let go of the dependency on the outside world for just a few minutes.* If you can appreciate the value of true, deep, purposeful concentration, then carve out a block of time, preferably right after you wake up in the morning and just before you fall asleep, when you consciously and deliberately let go of the concerns, the limitations of the outside, everyday environment.

Turn in and tune into another station within yourself. Give your mind a breather. Breathe quietly and deeply. Clear the movie screen in your mind. Make it blank, dark, and quiet. Then allow positive images to appear. See yourself walking down a long, lovely, quiet beach with the ocean rolling in at your feet. See yourself in the tranquillity of a mountain lake with sunny skies. See yourself standing before a client and making the sale easily, with good humor. See yourself as prosperous, happy, and active in a relaxed and purposeful way. Choose your mood for the day. Give yourself a mental breakfast of positive images — *then* go out and see what the world has to offer.

This is by far the best and most productive form of concentration — positive mental pictures for breakfast and your midnight snack. Your level of concentration depends upon you giving yourself the chance to quiet down and turn in. These few daily moments of pictorial concentration — *one picture is worth a thousand words* — will be worth their weight in gold. These few moments in the morning and in the evening will help you choose your thoughts for yourself instead of having other people, events, and circumstances choose them for you. You will not be concentrating *on* something as much as you will be concentrating *from* a perspective about yourself.

What you see will come true. If you can see it, you can do it. That is the real power of concentration. Can you see yourself thinking on your feet, meeting every circumstance "out there" with poise, calm, and assurance within?

PREPARATION

Almost everybody likes to win, to be a success, to be happy, productive, and prosperous. Almost everybody has the will to win, but few people have the *will to prepare*. Although many people in our society aspire to excellence, few people have the desire to work on themselves at the depths that are necessary to perform with excellence on a consistent basis.

For example, I once interviewed the president of a small food service company. He reported that his top salespeople made $75,000 a year, while the average salesperson made about $25,000. "What is the difference?" I asked, expecting a huge difference in education, talent, or contacts.

"Preparation," said the president. "When the man has a 9 a.m. presentation before a school board district that means hundreds of thousands of dollars, he gets to his location at 6:30 and sets up in a relaxed mood. That means getting up at 4 a.m. or so, but this man has the vision of what it means to his pocketbook and to his self-esteem to be number one in this company. He has the will to prepare, and enjoy himself in the process."

Preparation really means a willingness to take a chance, to change with new conditions, to look within for solutions that no one else wants to think about. Of course, there are good reasons not to make waves, to play it safe, to accept the benefits of the company in exchange for your own freedom and creativity. Yet, what we are aiming for here is *an incredible standard of excellence*. The exercises that follow are designed to raise your performance and your standard of living one (or more) notch higher. If you feel that you could express more of your talent, your creativity, and your own unique individuality, this will be an opportunity for you to tune in, turn on, and use "your big guns."

The major prerequisite for being a clear thinker and a dynamic speaker is a willingness to change, to listen, to turn *within* for the solution to your problems *out there*. Being a ready, willing, and able speaker means being a pioneer, one who seeks new ground to break. As a marketing director once reported to me, "the secret to success in the 1980s and 1990s is to develop new products. Those who will get ahead are those who think creatively and express themselves with confidence, vision, and clarity."

There is no better preparation than a deep, personal commitment to oneself. When you work to develop and refine your own unique talent, your own power of thinking and feeling in a positive manner, you unleash a tremendous creative force within your own system. When you work with yourself and stop getting in your own way with limiting thought, beliefs, and addictions to the external realities of your world, you begin to rise above your old limitations. You begin to become free.

And freedom is what is at stake here — freedom to think creatively, perform with excellence, and reap the rewards of top performance.

This book will give you positive tips and practical directions to prepare you to think on your feet and say what you mean in any and all situations. A good speaker, a decisive spokesperson, a creative thinker is always in large demand. This process of self-training does take a certain courage and willingness to let go of old habits and thought patterns. It will ask a constant enthusiasm for change and growth on your part. But as you begin to practice the principles and see how they work for you to help you achieve your personal and professional goals, you will notice a new confidence and an eagerness to relate to people. The same situations that used to make you nervous, anxious, and fearful will be transformed into opportunities for financial, social, and personal reward.

Thinking on your feet, with spontaneity, purpose, and style, will give you a slight edge in your business and social life. A slight edge is all you really need to make your mark and prosper through your talents. There is room at the top — especially for those who can rise to the occasion with grace, confidence, and self-regulation.

2

The Slight Edge Technique

In major league baseball, a batter who gets two hits out of every ten times at bat is called a .200 hitter. Within a very short period of time, a .200 hitter is "fired" by the management and sent back to the minor leagues, and, unless the batting average improves, he soon is looking for a job outside of baseball.

But a hitter who gets three hits out of every ten times at bat is a .300 hitter and considered a great success. In the current market, .300 hitters are often paid hundreds of thousands of dollars a year — with long-term, no-cut contracts worth millions and millions of dollars.

So, .300 hitters are in a far different class than .200 hitters. All for one more success out of every ten tries. Not a big edge, just a slight edge. Yet, it makes a great difference.

Because it is so easy to tell the winners from the losers in the sports field, another example can also illustrate the slight edge principle. In the 1975 pro golf tour, Jack Nicklaus was the top money winner for the year. He won $298,149 by shooting an average score per round of 69.88. Don January was listed number thirty on the money winners, making $69,034 by shooting an average score per round of 71.48. Arnold Palmer was number thirty-six in ranking, winning $59,017 by shooting a 71.77 average score per round. Jim Simons was number fifty winning $47,724 with an average score per round of 71.89.

The difference between numbers one and fifty – between Nicklaus and Simons – was less than two strokes per round! But the dollar difference was almost $250,000! The slight edge turned into six figures on the bottom line. And who ever heard of Jim Simons?

At the professional level of competition, talent is there. Everybody is talented. The winners are the ones who can express their talents under pressure. When the heat is on, the perpetual, perennial winners are the ones who had a *slight edge,* not a big edge. If you can have one more success out of every ten tries or if you can cut your "extra strokes" down by one or two, you can raise yourself to the top of your profession.

You don't need to infuse yourself with more talent. You have all the talent you will ever have right now within yourself. You cannot go out and get a transfusion of talent, but you can develop your talents by practicing your technique.

Talent is not the distinguishing factor for success! *Technique is.* The question is, what do you do to express your talent under pressure?

Those people who consistently make the sale, manage people, and come up with the creative ideas do not have a great edge in talent as much as they have a method of working. They invest time in themselves in such a way as to make the most out of what they have. In everyday, normal business, social, and professional life, the "slight edge" comes from an ability to turn yourself on when there are good reasons to turn yourself off.

You can gain the slight edge by thinking on your feet and communicating at the moment of pressure. The slight edge is a matter of *presence of mind* — knowing what you are doing at the moment you are doing it. It is the ability to come up with the right word at the right time in the moment of crisis.

Some people believe that this ability is just a knack that some have, and others don't. But that is not true. If you can speak at all and come up with what you should have said ten minutes after a crucial conversation, you can think on your feet. As with most pressure situations like thinking on your feet, getting to the point, and having a positive impact on those around you, the will to prepare, practice, and persevere are more important than natural talent. As the successful college basketball coach Bobby Knight says, "Lots of people have the will to win. Champions have the will to prepare."

Thinking on your feet and rising to the occasion of pressure are very much like learning a musical instrument, sailing a boat, or driving a car. Some people who have mastered the art of being themselves while the heat is on compare their act to learning a new language. At first, you really have to want to do it. You have to see for yourself the tremendous advantage of being able to think, speak, and act under pressure. You need to feel a stirring within yourself to surpass yourself. You have to feel the fire of desire — the desire to make more money, to have mental and emotional freedom, and a sense of complete independence.

Are you now in a position where you could use a "slight edge technique" — a simple but effective way to increase your productivity, use your creativity, and demonstrate greater control over the variables in your life?

Do you have a talent for communications that is somehow not being expressed to the degree that it could?

Is there room to develop and refine your natural speaking talent — so you can radiate confidence, enthusiasm, and expertise no matter where you are or what is happening around you?

Can you see the tremendous advantage of being able to think quickly and communicate more effectively under pressure?

The following technique has been developed during the course of hundreds of effective-speaking workshops and has proven successful for thousands of people who have invested time in themselves before 9 a.m. and after 5 p.m. to develop their own speaking and thinking skills. It is called the Slight Edge Technique because it develops presence of mind, inward control, and imaginative flashes of insight in everyone who enjoys the efforts.

Have fun with it. Get the basic idea. Take it where you want to go. Just as you can win a greater sense of freedom in a car or a sailboat, gain the same sense of freedom by seeing yourself winning the slight edge. Don't play the victim of circumstances. Enjoy these efforts. Fill in the spaces with your own feelings, ideas, and visions. Demonstrate the slight edge wherever you go.

LEARNING THE SLIGHT EDGE TECHNIQUE

The Slight Edge Technique consists of doing two things every day. Just as you wake up, dress, eat, go to work, bathe, and sleep, all you have to do is add two simple activities to your daily routine.

Essentially, what you will be doing is putting a different frame around the picture of your day. Have you ever noticed that a painting or photograph can look totally different if another frame is placed around it? The quality of the entire visual experience changes if you put a wooden or stainless steel frame around the original. The picture remains the same, but it looks different because of what you added to it.

A motivational research corporation was once hired to find out why some people of equal talent proved to have different levels of success. The research group interviewed a number of people who had similar qualifications. All had an adequate education, years of experience, and some kind of family structure to support. On paper, they looked very much the same. Yet some were struggling with an average, middle-of-the-road salary, while others were making six figures and feeling very good about themselves in many ways. Some were working for others, but the most successful people were working for themselves. No matter who was signing their paychecks, the people who demonstrated superior standards of living all had the feeling that they were *working for themselves*. Their jobs afforded them the opportunity to grow as individuals. More important than their product or their company policy was their own personal growth.

The survey showed that the top three percent of the people polled did two things. First, they bought a blank notebook or journal and communicated with themselves at two very special times of the day. In the early morning just after rising and in the late evening just before retiring, they would sit quietly and "talk" to themselves by writing down some ideas and feelings in their own book. The secret to success was that *they wrote their own book!* They invested time in their own thinking and feeling. They put a positive frame around their day by clearing their mind and picturing what they wanted to happen rather than what they did not want to happen.

They made these two basic efforts part of their daily routine:

1. They would sit quietly and calmly right after waking— no radio or TV blaring — and write down their *idea for the day.*

2. They would *visualize* themselves acting upon the idea they had written down.

What they wrote down was *not* a list of who to phone or letters to write or appointments to keep. It was an *idea* that they would plant in their minds like a seed. This idea had nothing to do with other people out there, but had everything to do with how to *respond* to people, places, and things out there.

These few quiet moments set the stage for the rest of the day. An idea was planted consciously and deliberately in the subcon-- scious mind that would then give direction and guidance under pressure in the environment. This basic idea for the day can color and influence every event that happens out there.

For example, a person might have decided that today *I am going to relax under pressure.* Perhaps this person knew that he was going to encounter very irritating and irritable people on his business rounds. Therefore, he selected a basic idea to prepare himself to meet those people. Then, he actually wrote the idea down on paper, as if the blank book were his own mind. Since it was blank, he could write down whatever he preferred. He chose his basic idea for the day, then impressed it on the book in his own handwriting.

Then he repeated the words and the idea to himself several times until he felt that he "got it." In a sense, he was feeding the subconscious computer a program that would cover all contingencies. (Chapter Four contains more examples to illustrate the kind of thought that may cover everything that happens during the day; here we just want to underline the thought that writing down the idea made a tremendous difference.)

Those people who wrote their ideas in a book had a record

of their own thinking and a means of review. The nightly, weekly, monthly review of their own books showed them in a very practical manner which basic "background" thoughts worked and which ones did not. The better they were able to see the effects of their own thinking on the outside world around them, the better able they were to choose the right idea for the right occasion, much as one would dress in an appropriate but different manner to meet different people.

Their ideas were very much like a suit of clothes. They dressed up their minds in much the same way they would dress up their bodies. The clearer, simpler, and more precise the basic thought, the more effective were their words, gestures, and actions. Then, after quietly selecting a thought for the day instead of settling for one, they would make the second basic effort of the Slight Edge Technique — visualizing the idea in action.

Since the mind is a personal screening room, you can flash on the screen any picture you want to. So the slight edge man in our example would see himself meeting with the irritable people and maintaining composure. He would picture himself in the environment where he expected to be and would see the meeting ending positively — the way he preferred. Instead of worrying or picturing what might go wrong or seeing the people as a problem, he made a mental picture of success. Since a picture is worth a thousand words and since the subconscious is a pictorial medium — we dream in pictures — a few minutes were taken *consciously* to talk to the subconscious in the language it most easily understands.

In other words, the slight edge people in the survey communicated with themselves at a depth level in a regular way. They cleared the mental field so the spontaneous idea could "land!" They set into motion what they wanted to happen instead of reacting blindly to the stimulations all around them.

Holding the picture of success for a few moments, they then *let it go*. They cleared the movie screen of all pictures and wordy thoughts. They took a few minutes of *total silence*, in an atmosphere of peace and calm, perhaps took a few deep breaths, and got the feeling that what they wanted to happen was *already in motion*. Instead of hurrying, worrying, or scurrying around the house in the morning, they consciously and deliberately took a few quiet moments for themselves because they intuitively knew the power of their own thinking and mental pictures.

The main point to grasp here is that you are *a living*

magnet. You attract to you the kind of experience that you are thinking about consciously or unconsciously. If you want to be free enough to talk with that irritable person or annoying relative, to strike a common truce and become compatible, you need to set that positive picture in your own mind.

See yourself as having difficulty, and you will greatly increase your chances of experiencing that difficulty. *You prepare your own way by the nature of your own thought patterns.* How you see yourself is what you will call to yourself. Knowing this, those who demonstrated the slight edge gave themselves nourishing thoughts for breakfast. As many people start their day with a dose of bad news or thumping music when the alarm goes off, it is also possible to feed your mind another kind of food.

Choose your idea for the day. See yourself acting on it. Release the idea into the subconscious by sitting quietly and relaxed — *then* go about your business.

During the day, the slight edge people of the survey would go about their rounds, taking care of their chores and duties, making a special effort to keep their idea conscious and active. With practice, they did not even have to try to remember what their idea for the day was. As the subconscious mind becomes used to being "fed" in the morning, it will ingest and incorporate the thoughts much as the physical body digests cereal, eggs, or toast.

After practicing the written thought for the day and the picture in the mind, the basic thought will be "there" — *as a presence.* A presence of mind. This presence of mind is what gives the practitioners "the slight edge." It comes from within, as that intangible but very real quality. It comes through as a spirit, a good will, a tolerance for the shortcomings of others, and a willingness to express a higher point of view under pressure.

As you begin to plant the idea in your mind by writing it in your book, you will slowly but surely feel the idea taking root in your system. If you begin, for example, deliberately to think *before* you react or respond, you will have the power of the idea working for you. You can better control yourself even in the most trying, difficult situation because you will be working from the inside out. You can control your own emotional temperature. You can demonstrate the thermostat consciousness. You can regulate your response by the power of your own thoughts. You do not have to let anybody "do it" to you. This one morning activity will soon show you the power of your own thinking. And this is the fundamental insight upon which all the other speaking techniques are built.

You always have a choice of how you respond. The slight edge is a function of remembering and practicing that power of choice. So, during the day, the slight edge people practiced their presence of mind. Before each meeting, they reminded themselves to act on their basic idea for the day; at night they would again take a few quiet minutes to review their day in light of their idea. Sitting quietly, they would look back over the day, in the sense of looking *over* it. Did they act on the idea in the meeting with that top executive? Did the idea guide their response with the grouchy clerk or secretary? "Did I really do what I intended to do?" they asked themselves.

If the answer was *yes*, they wrote down a brief description of the encounter with the particular person and gave themselves a pat on the back. First they would look for their successes and give themselves credit for the moments when they truly acted with presence of mind. Then they would look for the moments when they went "unconscious" — when the outside worked in and changed their emotional or intellectual temperature. They looked for the circumstances that reduced them to being thermometers — when they simply registered the temperature around them.

Citing those moments, they would ask themselves a crucial question — what got in my way? Or, in other words, what prevented me from acting on my idea and executing my intention?

Sometimes it would be a particular person. Other times, it would be a lack of time. Sometimes, the secretary would make a mistake. *Most times,* it was simply a lack of consciousness.

The most interesting and intriguing conclusion made by the *most* successful people was that *they got in their own way.* When something went wrong, it was mainly because they lost their own presence of mind. As they wrote down descriptions of both successes and "failures" in their own private journal, patterns began to emerge. It became easier to see when the idea for the day was present and effective, or absent and ineffective. By reviewing their answers and descriptions, it became possible to have an insight into the way *mind* works.

It also became possible to see that when the "idea for the day" was present, it was easier to communicate with other people. When the basic thought for the day guided the actions, it was easier to be spontaneous and free. Once the background thought was the guide, ideas came and words were expressed that were right for the occasion. When the idea was present, feelings were positive. When the idea was present, there seemed to be a guiding light, an intuitive flow, a spontaneous flash. When the idea was absent, there were delays, disappointments, and detours.

Over a period of time, writing their own book became their most important priority. The best book you could possibly read about self-realization and success is the one you write yourself. More important than what happens to you or around you is what happens *in you*.

It might be of interest to read some of the feedback from people who have practiced the Slight Edge Technique and kept their journals up-to-date over a period of time. Although the specific incidents of individuals obviously varied, certain common themes and variety of experience began to take place. There were many startling revelations and mutual stumbling blocks, but all who kept up this practice reported that they came in touch with their own *original voice*. Here are some suggestions to consider before you start the technique, to get a feel for what might happen in your own life.

1. *You will run up against the inertial patterns within your own consciousness.* The most difficult part is getting started, making the time to sit quietly in the morning and in the evening. There will be a pull toward the outside world to get things done and maintain your usual habit.

2. *Even with great motivation, you will miss or skip a few days.* In your book, there will be a couple of blank pages. You can either use the missed days as an excuse to stop or a motivation to continue. You will soon see that your book will not get written by itself. The journal is a definite choice you make about your own affairs — nobody else is really in the picture. You do have a choice.

3. *The evening review period is more important than the morning statement of intention.* If you review your day carefully, calmly, objectively, cleverly, the idea for the next day will suggest itself without you having to worry about it or invent one. The idea for the following day is right there in the events of this day. The message is there. By reviewing at night, you can set an idea in motion, and "sleep on it." This allows the great creative unconscious some time to integrate the idea into the deeper realms of your psyche. The seed idea for Monday morning is really planted on Sunday evening.

4. *As you read over your own entries in a regular way, you will soon be able to "read between the lines" and identify patterns of*

unconscious thought and behavior. As you make these unconscious patterns more conscious, you will naturally and organically develop presence of mind. It is a matter of seeing and dissolving the blocks. You will have many moments of *recognition* — some painful, some joyous, some startling, all revealing.

5. *You will come to the point when you enjoy the quiet time and your relationship with your book.* At first, you may feel it is an obligation, as yet another duty and responsibility that you *have* to do. You will come to a great turning point when you sincerely want to take this time and write for yourself. Write in the book as if you were talking to a good friend — because you want to. The journal is of little help if it becomes or remains an obligation — something you feel you *ought* to do.

6. *Read your entries aloud.* Part of your daily review should be the reading aloud of your entire entry from the previous day. About once a week or every two weeks, go back and read your book from page one to the present. Read over your book as if it were written by somebody else.

7. *Do not tell a lot of people what you are doing.* Keep this quiet time a secret. As soon as you tell people about it, they will often try to do something to interfere. You also set yourself up as a target if you start to tell people that you are in the process of changing and getting better. They will tend to expect major differences when, in fact, the changes are subtle and attitudinal in the early stages.

8. *Use your book in whatever way you want.* It is there for impulsive, spontaneous expression. It is there as an outlet for "wild and crazy" thoughts and feelings, for great ideas and visions of what you could be or want to do. Play with the entries — make this a "dream book."

9. *You will become convinced that you have a special unique talent.* It is your major mission in life to express that potential within. The quiet moments give you the opportunity to connect with that inner dimension, which then acts as a guide in your outside affairs. If you become anxious, annoyed, or irritable, all you have to do is be still and know that you are connected to this inner source of peace and confidence. The quiet time in the morning and in the evening with focused consciousness will lead to greater peace, calm, and confidence in the affairs of the world.

10. *The journal soon becomes a part of yourself* — like a

member of your family that cares especially about you and how you are doing. It will feel like an older brother, a generous aunt, a wise grandfather, or grandmother. Many people begin to "talk to" their journal as if it were a loving, caring, understanding person. It is a very good sign when your journal takes on a life of its own.

11. *There is nothing quite comparable to the feeling of finishing your first book.* If you practice regularly, the pages will soon fill up, almost without even trying. You will have written your first book, and it will be an original. It will not be for publication probably, but there very well might be some ideas or concepts that you can use in the public marketplace.

12. *Your goals for the future and your lifelong task will become more and more apparent.* There seems to be an inner pattern of action that is inside every person. You will become more aware of your place, your right profession, and your great talent as you keep your book and make quiet time for yourself. You will develop a dialogue with your "higher self," which will influence and permeate everything you do.

13. *All you are responsible for are the basic efforts.* In your quiet time of meditation and journal writing, you do not have to *make* anything happen. Rather, you *let* something happen. You do not have to *try* to write anything. If you are truly quiet and listen to "the silence," thoughts will come to you automatically. There is something in you that *wants* to come to the surface. Your job is to cooperate.

The major difficulty with the Slight Edge Technique is that you will be less likely to conform with outside expectations and demands. This can be a problem if you live in a highly structured, rigid, and demanding environment. The efforts of this exercise will naturally and organically develop your sense of yourself at a very deep level. You might very well find yourself wanting to make a change in your immediate environment.

The practice of this Slight Edge Technique will automatically place you in contact with a "higher world" — one not subject to the stress and strain of the consumer market. It leads to a state of mind that may be called "constructive discontent." Chances are you will not accept your past limitations as being part of your "nature." This technique will demonstrate to you over and over again that you are unique — very much an original.

You will want to express yourself. You will not be so

ready to allow the limitations of other people to become your criteria for behavior. You will become aware of a level of excellence within yourself that is truly remarkable and sensational. You will be motivated to think on your feet and say what you mean because you will be living more in the moment than in the past or in the future. You will have a relationship with yourself that far surpasses any you have had with other people out there in the world — although you will find yourself getting along with more people in your environment.

The Slight Edge Technique will help you relax and concentrate under pressure, so don't be surprised if the slight edge soon becomes a giant edge. The better you know yourself, the more you will like yourself, and the more you will attract other people and opportunity.

Then there are important questions to answer: Do I want the slight edge? Am I ready to expand and enlarge my circles of living? Do I really want to get better? Do I really want to go one notch higher? Am I ready for the challenges and opportunities of excellence? Am I ready to be myself?

You have all you need right now to be a success in the *express* business. You don't have to suppress, repress, or digress any more. You can and should express yourself — if only in your own book. The best way to gain confidence is to *set a short-term goal and execute it.*

Quiet time for oneself and one's journal is a short-term goal that is within the range of every person reading this book. All you are responsible for are the efforts.

3

The Attitude of Altitude

At first, it is not easy to see the relationship between investing ten quiet, relaxed, focused minutes a day and communicating with impact. Framing your day in a silent, positive way seems too simple a technique for the emergence of spontaneous, confident thought to flow through the normal exchanges with other people. But the truth of the matter is that quiet time for yourself taps depths in you that can be approached in no other way. *Thought is creative* — one way or the other. It is not the amount of time you invest, but what you do with that time that really counts.

In this exercise, effort is more important than intellectual assent. *All you are responsible for is the effort.* In this matter, persistence and perseverance are not mere cliches. They are constructive actions of mind that will affect your basic attitude of the day.

What you *will* develop through consistent effort may be called an *attitude of altitude,* an elevated perspective of looking at yourself and the circumstances in your life — from the highest point of view. When it comes to effective communications, nothing is more powerful than a belief in yourself. As you begin consciously to connect with the quiet center within yourself, you will begin to cultivate a tremendous faith in the power of the invisible over the visible, the power of your own thoughts over the circumstances in your life.

The goal of your ten golden minutes is an *altitude of thinking,* an elevated state of mind. Working with yourself and on yourself in the morning and evening will develop your belief and conviction in yourself. As you impress your great idea for the day on your subconscious mind, you will find that you are in touch with your quiet center for longer and longer periods of the day. Out there, "they" won't be able to push your anger, fear, or resentment button so easily. You will be better able to push your own buttons. At that point, your talent will begin to flow as smoothly as water runs from an unclogged faucet. You will always be connected to the source of great ideas — the superconscious mind.

The purpose of the Slight Edge Technique is to free you from self-limiting patterns of thought, a slave to what *has been* in your life. It doesn't matter what you have done in the past or what you have fed yourself about being unable to speak your mind in difficult situations in your public and personal life. Instead of being a *has been,* be a *could be.* To be totally "realistic," you have to let go of the past patterns and make way for your talent to come into expression. The truth is that most of us have not tapped the potential inside of us. The Slight Edge Technique, the S.E.T., is a positive treatment of yourself for the primary purpose of getting yourself out of your own way. The S.E.T. can and will clear out your consciousness and put you in touch with the source of your true power.

The Slight Edge Technique will give you a new *set* of internal controls. You will develop the "thermostat consciousness," regulating your own temperature from within through the power of your own ideas. Consistent practice of the S.E.T. will lead to four specific benefits:

1. *You will expand your consciousness.* You will become more aware of the power of your own conscious choice — that *you* control your reactions to things and people around you.

2. *You will clarify your thoughts and thereby your goals.* You will begin to see from the writings in your own book how your basic idea or thought pattern of the day actually shapes and forms what happens to you.

3. *You will remove the obstructions that have limited you in the past.* The greatest barriers we face are within our own mental households. As you consciously clear away resentment, worry, fear, and suspicion, you will open up ways of expressing your *original* talent.

4. *You will realize the presence of a creative spirit within.* As you relax and let go of your past limited thought patterns about your communications expertise, another dimension of yourself will shine through spontaneously. In your own book, written in your own hand, you will see how often you got in your own way. A careful study of your book will help you to be your own greatest asset. You won't beat yourself as much as you used to. The recognition of your self-limiting thought patterns will lead to affirmative action.

This elevation of thought will lead to a freedom of expression. Confidence beginning in thought and in positive visual pictures then filters into action. That is why you can never paste on good speaking techniques from the outside. There are no catch phrases or guaranteed jokes to warm up an audience or a client. First, there must be a refinement in consciousness within yourself and an expansion of your belief system before your words will flow smoothly and have a positive effect on any audience all the time. It takes practice and effort, but all you are responsible for is the effort.

The great lesson of the S.E.T. is that you can experience thinking on many levels at the same time. This elevated activity of thought is called *Multileveled Thinking* and develops a fundamental quality for success — presence of mind. By using three dimensions of your own mind, you focus and concentrate your talent toward a specific goal. In diagram form, these levels are:

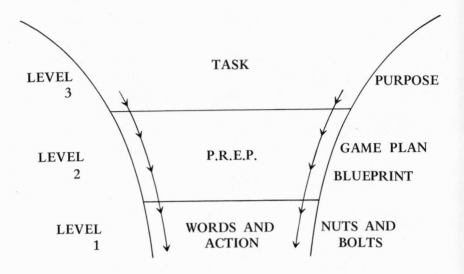

This funnel-shaped figure is essentially how your mind works when it comes to an effective exchange with others in your environment. When you begin with level three — the Task Level — you start with your idea or purpose. That will give substance to Level Two — the P.R.E.P. Level which gives form or organization to your original impulse. Level One — Words and Actions — is what you can experience with your senses. You work *down* from Level Three *through* Level Two into Level One. The abstract idea given shape and form manifests itself in action.

In any verbal exchange between any number of people, three levels of thought are available: Let us examine them more closely.

LEVEL THREE – TASK

On the highest level, *a purpose could be communicated.* It is interesting to note that the original meaning of the word *communication* was "common union." That became shortened to "communion," which then became "communication." The best of all possible communications takes place between two parties when there is an acknowledged purpose of common union, where there is an exchange that benefits both parties.

In any given exchange where there is a mutual benefit for both speaker and listener, there can be a conscious intention that guides, shapes, and gives direction to the words. When an idea is present in the form of a conscious purpose, the intention will guide you to find the right word from a higher perspective.

This highest level of purpose-intention-common union is called the Task Level. Here is where you take some time and *give yourself something specific to do,* a definite goal to accomplish. Here you clarify in your own mind *what you wish to happen as a result of speaking.* When this visual picture of how you prefer your words to impact on another person is clear and sharp in your own mind, you will have level three – the highest and most powerful level – working for you.

The best way for you to clarify your own particular task in any meeting, presentation, or spontaneous exchange with another is to ask yourself the following questions:

What effect do I want to have on this audience?

What do I want the audience to do as a result of my word?

Unfortunately, many people do not take the time to clarify their purpose before they speak or make a presentation. *They do not put the audience into their mental picture.* Projecting their basic picture of their own insecurity on their actions, they become too concerned with the rote recitations of facts and figures. They are very worried about what the audience is thinking about them. They want to be right, good, cool, instead of really *exchanging* a part of themselves with another person. When Level Three is not clearly in focus, your words will arbitrarily hit or miss the mark.

Under pressure, tension, or anxiety, this is the first level of consciousness to go blank. Since this is the most mental, invisible, and intangible level, it is the most difficult to keep in mind when the business tasks and chores of the day demand attention. When you lose sight of this level of consciousness, you work from the outside in and give away the power of your purpose. You lose your presence of mind.

When a speaker in any audience allows the basic fear of

that audience to get in the way, the task of the action flies out the window. Without a clear and definite purpose, your words will tend to be repetitive and purposeless. So, what is your task in speaking your words? What is your purpose? What do you want the other person *to do after you finish speaking?*

It is important to see that any resentment, resistance, or anxiety first affects level three of your mind. Your own emotional and mental state gets in the way of your purpose if it is marked by self-doubt, self-criticism, self-concern. But if you focus your attention on *what you can give to the other person,* you do *yourself* a tremendous favor. By thinking of the other, you unleash powerful positive forces within yourself. That is precisely why inside control is so very important and vital to good communications.

Especially because your audience may also be under pressure to produce, displaying a certain mental and emotional tightness of their own, you have to take it upon yourself to know, *really know,* the purpose of your communication. They might have their own concerns and worries, so they might not be receptive to you or your ideas. If you do not have a clear picture of what you want to accomplish, you can easily be thrown off track.

Heed this warning and see how often it applies to yourself in your everyday exchanges. *Many people do not clarify the mutual purpose in any given verbal exchange.* Caught in the unconscious habit of working from the outside in, they let their emotions – usually some degree of paranoia and inferiority – be ruled by what happens to them. They speak very often without consciousness of the effect they are having on the other person. They become too concerned with getting their words (often complaints and excuses) out – not with building a bridge with the listener.

From the highest, most profitable point of view, there is one purpose and *only one purpose* in saying anything. That purpose is to *build a bridge* – to make a positive connection with the other person. If you are not consciously building a bridge, you might very well be burning a bridge. If you do not really consider the effect of your words on the other, you will be seen as self-centered and insensitive. You will be perceived as "knowing it all" and difficult to get along with so your information will be pushed aside and ignored. Not because of what you say, but because of how you are saying it.

Communication is a two-way street. There needs to be a common union, a mutually beneficial purpose, or else it is better not to say anything at all. Some poor speakers say too little; others are poor because they say too much. Both types share the same basic problem — a lack of conscious purpose. Both say words just to say words — as if words could fill in the empty space in themselves. So before you do anyting else, take some time to clarify your task. Visualize your audience. See that person responding and benefiting by the very least of your words. Be sure you have your mutual purpose in mind — and let this purpose be your guide.

The Task Level of Multileveled Thinking is not easy to keep in mind all the time, but it is a very worthwhile goal to shoot for. Those who neglect to clarify their vision and purpose in their everyday communications often take life as it comes rather than initiating their own individual brand of talent. Soon they are always on the outside looking in. This is a natural psychic law — those who rise to the top of any field get there first in their thinking. With their own mental household in order and in shape, results are sure to follow.

You will *never* have a slump when you allow the task to work down through your emotions and your words. When you are fired with a task and definite purpose, you shine with enthusiasm and positive attitude. But to speak and act with purpose, *you* must create that purpose for yourself. At the highest levels, nothing can be left to chance.

LEVEL TWO — THE P.R.E.P. FORMULA

Level Two of consciousness that could be working in any situation of communication is called the P.R.E.P. Formula. This is the level of *organization* where you set a game plan or sketch out a blueprint to achieve your purpose.

Level Two is called into play when you have clarified your purpose in visual pictures and now want to translate that mental image into action. The first step to win the game or make the sale is to give yourself a step-by-step outline to follow when the pressure is on.

P.R.E.P. is a code word for preparation. The team or individual who has clarified both the purpose and the game plan built for a specific, target audience is the one likely to have it all in the end.

In sports and business, the winner is the one who can make the opponent play his or her game. In personal affairs, the best relationships are those based on mutual consideration and unity of purpose. The person who most clearly and intelligently fulfills the considered game plan usually wins the point, makes the sale, or gains the opportunity to grow into another role in a higher, more elevated position.

Once you know that you want a desk and a chair to write a book, for example, you can then take specific steps to buy the materials, draw up the blueprints, and create an environment as you want it to be to express your inner self and your deepest talent. You use your inner life, your levels of mind, to bring an abstract, invisible, intangible idea into being. This act of making something out of "nothing," creating a product from an original idea, is called *creativity*. In this sense, we are all creative, and we can all demonstrate a creative process in our daily lives.

But first you must have the picture of a desk and chair. You could go out and buy wood, hammer, and nails, but without a blueprint, all the nuts and bolts would have no focus, no meaning, no direction. You could hammer and saw for hours and days and not build anything. Without an organizing principle, and without an orderly picture in your own mind, your product and efficiency will be haphazard at best.

So when it comes to answering an unexpected question on the spot or winning a point in a crucial meeting against an opponent, what is your inner game plan? Do you have a blueprint or formula to organize your thoughts on the spot, when you don't have the time or the opportunity to refer to notes or research what you say? What do you do when you have to organize your material in a concise, precise, logical order in a second or two?

The organizing principle of effective speaking can be focused and crystallized into the P.R.E.P. formula:

P = Point of view.
R = Reasons why.
E = Evidence or examples to illustrate your point of view.
P = Point of view restated, leading to the ACTION you
     want your audience to take.

The P.R.E.P. Formula is a way to organize your thoughts on the spot, even if you have not been given much time to prepare. It is one of the greatest tools in refining your ability to think on your feet, one that becomes smoother and smoother as you use it in daily conversation or in preparation for a formal presentation. When you begin to think in this format, you will never have to worry about saying too much or too little. All you have to know is where you are in the formula.

The P.R.E.P. Formula is like a checklist. If you were flying your own plane, you would pick a destination and check over all your equipment *before* you took off. While still on the ground, you would check your instruments, your fuel supply, your landing gear, your radio. You would have a routine or game plan that you would enact *every time* you flew. You would not take anything for granted or leave anything to chance. You would prepare before the flight so that you could react spontaneously to any emergency while actually in flight.

The P.R.E.P. is a thought process *before* you make your presentation or answer a difficult, challenging question. The more you use it, the quicker it becomes, and although we will devote the entire fifth chapter to exercises to make it more real and practical for you, it would be appropriate here to give you a taste of how it works.

P

In many spontaneous and formal presentations alike, the speaker often has not clarified his or her *point of view,* or opening remark that will make an impact and set the stage for the rest of the material to follow. If you are asked a question that demands an immediate response, take a moment to establish your point of view, or *overview,* on the issue. This is the first step in the P.R.E.P. Formula — the opening response. *Point of view* means zeroing in on what you really mean to say, or else there is a suspicious gap between your words and your inner activity. Be known for what you are saying, not what you are not saying. Those people who win a reputation for *not saying* the most important material soon have to play hide-and-seek power games with all those around.

R.

To back up your point of view, have some clear reasons why you think that way. A point of view without clear reasons why is merely an opinion. Anyone can have an opinion, but a strong point of view always transcends a mere opinion. There are considered reasons and facts to back up a point of view — only a personal prejudice is behind an opinion.

E.

Your supporting *evidence* is part three of the P.R.E.P. Formula. Here, names, dates, times, and places, as well as general economic and world conditions, are cited specifically. Here you show that you have a definite set of experiences to back up your words. Your evidence or *examples to illustrate* should never be abstract or speculative. If they are, you might need to rethink your point of view, as it might be only an opinion.

P.

To insure your desired effect on your listener, **restate your point of view**, asking for the **ACTION** you would like your audience to take. This part of the P.R.E.P. puts the audience firmly in the closing. A good speaker always asks for an action — a specific response from the audience.

      Years and years in training seminars working at all levels with people from varied backgrounds have revealed an amazing, startling, and even shocking fact! Most people do not have a point of view on their material. Often, they do not know which facts and figures they have gathered are most important or crucial to their presentation. Without an overview, they begin to present the facts with no specific logic, form, or order. On many occasions they have not considered their audience or where the unexpected question was coming from. Without taking a moment to think through an organizing scheme like the P.R.E.P., they say the first thing that pops into their heads, and they wind up thinking about what they should have said ten minutes after the meeting is over.

      Without a firm inner organizing principle, you can very often be at the mercy of the unexpected. The P.R.E.P. Formula will give you a method of *thinking through* problems or issues in a logical, concise manner. Even if your audience does not agree with your point of view, they will at least recognize that you have one and were able to come up with an intelligent answer without preparation.

      As soon as you begin to think vertically, that is, with Levels Three and Two active and present in your consciousness during your activities on the outside, you begin to rise above the horizontal plane of circumstance. As soon as you elevate your thinking beyond Level One, you have an experience of "altitude." You bring into play a dimension of yourself where you allow no one to do *it* to you. As you raise your thinking one notch higher by putting it through the P.R.E.P. checklist, the external, material, and environmental conditions around you change for the better.

You are on top of the situation.

Do you have a game plan for your next telephone call, whatever it might be? Even though you do not know who will be calling you or when you will have to turn on your best self unexpectedly, you still can be prepared from the inside out when you practice the P.R.E.P. Formula. As you begin to think, write, and respond in the P.R.E.P., your words will have an inner logic and conciseness no matter what the issue or situation. They will be there, in you as a presence, when you practice on your own time.

The hard, cold fact of business, artistic, and professional life is that if you are not properly prepared to meet the difficult, unexpected crisis, someone else will be. If you do not have your instrument in tune physically, emotionally, and psychologically, someone else will. If you don't want to win the match by investing time to develop your craft from the inside out, someone else will. If you do not stand up, take the floor, and express yourself, someone else will. If you do not answer a question or provide a solution, someone else will. If you do not keep your eye fixed on a goal and work systematically toward a specific end, someone else will.

There's room at the top. Middle management is where it's crowded.

LEVEL ONE – NUTS AND BOLTS

Level One is the "nuts and bolts" dimension of Multileveled Thinking. The purpose defined and visualized, the game plan ordered and thought through, now it is time to fill in the preparation stage with action. Level One is what we actually see and hear in performance – the physical, visceral, visible *you*. It is the level that is most obvious because it exists in the tangible, sensational, three-dimensional world. It is also the level where most people get stuck.

In the act of communication, many people focus on *content* – finding the right word, the right statistic, the glib phrase to get over. Many believe if they do their technical homework and gather the current information and data, they will get their message across. Many reared in traditional education believe that the less of themselves they put into their information, the better the presentation. When they deliberately shut off their emotions, attitudes, and personal point of view, they have been taught that they are communicating in an effective manner.

Not true! Communication is the *exchange* of information, feelings, and spirits. The message must reach and *touch* the listener. It must make an emotional and personal impact if that listener is to take an action. We receive so much information during the course of a normal day that we become desensitized to a large degree. When information is simply information — dry, impersonal, one-dimensional fact — it *rarely* makes an impact.

Think of the most effective speakers you have experienced. What are their most outstanding qualities? What are they adding to their information to make their messages come alive? What are they *giving* that colors the facts of the matter with nuance, rhythm, and style?

The following traits seem to characterize dynamic, effective communicators:

1. They are relaxed, confident, and "into" their subject.

2. They display presence of mind — a deep sense of themselves as individuals. They are not afraid to be themselves.

3. They speak simply and directly *to* — not *at* — their audience. They are open to the spoken and unspoken feelings of those in their presence.

4. They have command of their material. They have *interpreted* their facts and figures. They have organized their material in a concise, logical, precise manner.

5. They enjoy the opportunity to communicate.

6. They are not afraid to play with and have a good time with their content. They *use* their material, instead of being a slave to it.

7. Long after you forget what they said, you remember *how* they said it. The most memorable part of the message was the *quality* of presentation.

In other words, you must do your professional homework and gather all the appropriate facts, figures, and statistics that need to be delivered to any audience. But you also must add your own personal quality to these objective facts. Your presentation is *not complete* until you color your words with your own individual personality.

More often than not, content gets in the way of effective communication. When people worry about getting their content "right," they often ignore the other dimensions of effective presentations. Nothing is more boring than a recitation of the facts and figures without attitude or feeling. Most people *report* information without making it personal and real to themselves — accounting for the feeling of separation from their work — and then wonder why the listener did not act on the information presented. The reason is because the audience did not *want* to.

Chapter Six describes and illustrates how to merge and blend content with personal style, but here we should know that *words alone do not make an impression.* If not backed with feeling and purpose, words mean nothing. Talk is cheap. Buzz phrases are a dime a dozen. The surface sayings and the current cliches of language are old hat and old-fashioned.

The effective communicator is always a pioneer, a trail-breaker because he or she allows the feeling of the moment to color all content. Having done the research and preparation work about the subject, he or she adds personal originality to the presentation. This speaker takes the stage by first preparing his or her own mental attitudes. He or she sees speaking in public, whether to an audience of one, ten, or one hundred, as an opportunity to express to the *outside* what is happening on the *inside*.

All effective communicators in the various circles of professional, public, and personal life are in the *express* business. They do not suppress, repress, or regress. They express the depth levels of themselves, knowing that what they are on the inside is good, right, transcendent of any limitations on the outside. They enjoy the creative process that *ends* in the verbal expression. They allow the spontaneity of the moment to take over and give their words an immediacy and urgency. It is important for them to speak, or else they keep silent.

The most important insight into Level One, the nuts and bolts dimension, is that you work *from the inside out*. The more you worry about your content and getting your words "right," the more the communicative channels will be blocked off. The more you let yourself and your fears of critical judgment get in your way, the more inhibited you will be about *everything*. The more you concentrate solely on your content, the less of yourself will flow through.

But the *you* is what counts in comm-*you*-nication. Without that original, spontaneous, creative *you* — the one that transcends outer limitations, judgments, and restrictions — you are only a carbon copy of someone else.

The pain, fear, and anxiety that many people feel when they have to think on their feet in front of a professional audience only means that there is something inside crying out for expression. By reading this book and growing through the suggested exercises, you are on the verge of a great breakthrough. No matter what your present level of success, by practicing the Slight Edge Technique and Multileveled (vertical) Thinking, you will be tapping a vast reservoir of imagination and intuition.

As you practice focusing in and holding a visual picture of your own potential success as a dynamic, effective communicator at the two quiet times of the day, these pictures will stay with you as an inner guide. During the pressured times of the day, the same outside forces that used to push you and pull you around in opposite directions will no longer have the power over your inner life. The key here is to keep your balance from within. The person who keeps an inner equilibrium, who thinks on several levels at the same time, will invariably be the winner.

So emotion can work for or against you. No matter what level of play, when talent and experience are about even, control of yourself will be the deciding factor. Remember that your external affairs are always a reflection of your internal state of mind. A positive relationship with yourself will balance your talent, technique, and character.

> TALENT *is what you have inside, given as potential.*
>
> TECHNIQUE *is what you do to develop what you have.*
>
> CHARACTER *is what you learn from experience to apply to your own personal growth.*

You are born with talent. Technique comes out of a conscious choice and discipline that awakens a deeper, higher dimension within yourself. Character is the application of what you know under pressure.

> *Fortunate are those who know what to do.*
>
> *Blessed are those who do do.*

The next three chapters develop and refine each level of Multileveled Thinking to illustrate how, when, and why they work in everyday life. If you are to help yourself to be a better speaker and a more confident communicator, you have to see the possibility of doing what was impossible before. The expanded sense of who you are, what you are, and where you are will always translate into action. The invisible always becomes visible.

The "attitude of altitude" is seeing yourself from the highest point of view. This nonverbal word, your basic feeling about yourself, shapes all your experience, especially interpersonal communications. All progress depends on your desire to get better.

4

Background Thinking

Do you remember the first time you rode a bike, drove a car, or sailed a boat by yourself? It was probably a bit awkward having to coordinate all the elements, stay on center in balance, and be aware of all that was happening around you at the same time. If you are like most people, you were a bit tentative in the beginning, a little unsure of yourself, perhaps wondering if this particular feat could *ever* be accomplished.

But if you stayed with the bike, the car, or the boat, there invariably came a moment when you *got it* — when you caught the idea, got the feeling, and began to move out on your own. There you were, wobbling on the path, weaving on the road, bobbing on the water, when — whoosh — everything came together and you were doing it! You were riding, driving, sailing! You were in control of the experience. Everything was working as it should.

Of course, you probably fell off the bike a few times. Of course, in the early stages, you often hit the brake too hard. You may even have capsized the boat or tangled yourself in the lines trying to catch the wind at just the right angle when you first got out on the water. But, in the back of your mind, you knew that bike riding, car driving, or boat sailing could be done because you witnessed so many other people doing it — easily, effortlessly, enjoyably. Because it had been done, it could be done. In the beginning, there was a problem, a doubt, a fear, but over and above all the momentary diversions, there was the image or picture of how it could be when everything came together in one whole.

Speaking before a group, making a sales presentation, reporting to a superior on a sticky subject are much like riding a bike, driving a car, or sailing a boat. Although it is very difficult to explain or teach the technical aspects of speaking with confidence and thinking on several levels at the same time, it is possible to achieve — and there are so many people who can do it! Just as there are fundamental laws to "obey" and become conscious of while you are biking, driving, or sailing, there are fundamental laws to effective communications.

Once you are aware of these basic principles and get into them by effort and practice, they work for you. Once you find your balance on the bike, coordinate the gas, the steering wheel, the rearview mirror, and the other elements of driving or sailing, *you have something within you that can never, ever be taken away.* You may not have ridden a bike, driven a car, or sailed a boat for years, but once you have gained that knowledge — or feeling — you can go back and perform the feat in a very few minutes. Once you have it, you have it for life. The same is true with Multileveled Thinking. Once the lightbulb goes on, you have a quality that will always be with you, one you will be able to turn on any time you want to.

Just as you can take riding, driving, and sailing to any degree of proficiency you choose, so too can you polish your craft of creative, spontaneous communicating to the point where it can be your most important asset. Once you have a deep feeling for thinking on several levels at the same time and witness the tremendous surge of self-confidence that accompanies multileveled thought, you can take it as far out and as far up as you want. Because the mind has an infinite number of levels and dimensions, the more you refine your presence of mind, the more comes to you as you practice the principles of effective speaking. As there are people who raise the level of riding, driving, and sailing to a professional art, you can sharpen your communication skills to the point where you can attract money, opportunity, and even love by your ability to express yourself convincingly when the pressure is on.

At first, the concept of Multileveled Thinking is a formidable one for many people. Several people in training seminars have been heard to say, "I have enough trouble thinking on one level. Don't talk to me about three levels or more. I'll be happy just taking care of business in a steady way. The art of communications is a luxury. Just give the practical basics, please."

The purpose of this chapter is to simplify and clarify the Multileveled Thinking diagram by breaking it down level by level to make it more real, accessible, and practical. The most confusion usually centers around the highest level, the Task Level, because of many past associations with the word *task*. For many people, task has the connotation of duty or obligation. So when we speak of a "task," there sometimes is a withdrawal because the seminar participant does not want or need any more duties, obligations, or tasks to live up to during an already busy day.

When we use the word *task*, however, we really mean a level of mind and thinking that sets a goal and can see an end result. When the child or young adult has a picture of what constitutes riding a bike, driving a car, or sailing a boat, that child has a *task* in mind. In the background of the mind, there is a purpose, a goal, a result, a freedom of body, mind, and soul. The child, then, can and will withstand many falls and spills, even a few bumps and bruises, while learning to ride because there is a mental picture present. Once the child has the vision in the mind, the picture of how it could be, he or she will find the means to ride down the street to feel the freedom of doing something on his or her own.

This *background picture* or *background thought* is what is meant by "task." Without a clear picture of the final result or purpose, it is very easy to give up trying to ride, drive or sail. Unless the picture is clear and bright, it is very easy to become frustrated, annoyed, and irritated. Many people quit when they lose this background picture/thought because everything around them seems to give out the message that they *can't* or *shouldn't* continue. A badly scraped knee or wounded ego is sometimes sufficient reason not to get on the bike again or stand before a group and give a presentation.

The fear of what might go wrong or "what they are thinking about me" can easily get in the way of continued effort. Just as the child who is afraid to fall *will* fall, the communicator who has a fear of making a mistake *will* make a mistake. The tentative background thought will prefigure tentative performance. Although the child may give up the desire to ride a bike and find other interests in life, it is not so easy to give up the need or desire for effective communications and positive interpersonal relations. It does not matter what business or profession you are involved in. You will always have to express yourself and deal with other people if you hope to live a harmonious and prosperous life.

In that light, what is your background thought for the day? What is going on in the back of your mind while you are eating, driving to work, having lunch, meeting with a business associate, auditioning for a role? What is happening inside your head while everything else is revolving around you on the outside?

Especially when it comes to effective communications and thinking quickly to solve problems, *nothing is more important than your background thought of the moment.* The clearer and freer the background thought, the more decisive, dynamic, and effective will be your self-expression. The problem with many people in both beginning and advanced stages of the training is that their background thought for the day is often *not their own.* Like a song that keeps returning to mind, the background thought that governs and shapes their actions is one they acquired years ago, one that has been imprinted on the mind via a nasty, difficult, or embarrassing situation. In the back of many minds is the picture of failure — the feeling of "I can't speak to this person or get along with that group of people." The *I can't* consciousness is tremendously widespread and infectious. It is easier to suppress and repress rather than express in many daily situations because a paycheck is at stake. Many people do not say what they feel because of the boss or the way things are "done around here."

In essence, many people allow their jobs, their parents, or even their grandparents do their background thinking for them. Ancient attitudes and archaic points of view get in the way of spontaneous expression more than anything else to block the creative, spontaneous flow of thought in normal exchanges between people. Seen in this light, prejudices, fears, and hostile attitudes hurt the person who holds them more than anyone else. You will get in your own way if your background thoughts and pictures are critical, resentful, or negative. When you do not get the kind of responses you want in your external environment, you would probably do very well to check out your internal background thinking.

There are several "background thoughts" that have proven very effective for all those who need to communicate with many different kinds of people in many ways on many levels on a regular basis. Especially if you are an actor, a salesperson, a manager, or an artist, the success of your idea, your product, or your service will ultimately depend on your ability to express yourself in a positive way. What you say is important, but *how* you say it could very well determine how it will be received by your audience. These background thoughts will develop an attractive quality in your attitude, your manner, and your style of presentation. Your content will be your own and will vary from business to business and from circumstance to circumstance. But your background thought needs to remain consistent, on target, on beam, on center for you truly to get your message across. You can always get a reading on how you are coming across by the actions your listener takes after you finish speaking.

PROGRESSIVE
BACKGROUND THOUGHTS

Relax Under Pressure

Imagine yourself in a tight pinch with your boss, colleague, best friend, or even your lover. Suppose that this person is angry, hostile, bitter, and nasty — with you as the target. Imagine that for some reason beyond your immediate control, this person is ranting and raving, yelling and screaming, or withdrawn in a cold and deadly silence. The other person is coming down hard on you, and it's very obvious that the person's background thought is extremely negative.

What has *your* background thought been in the past in such situations? While the other person was doing his or her act and number on you, what has been going on in your own mind? Have you been upset, defensive, silently muttering to yourself about how horrible this person is? Have you thought one thing and said another? Have you swallowed your background thought and feeling and let the situation develop as a passive bystander?

This is a very important illustration of the basic principle of effective communication. *More important than what is happening around you or to you is what is happening in you.* At a crucial moment like this, when the pressure is really on, you have an extremely interesting and creative decision to make. *What do you want your background thought to be?* What do you want to be happening *in* you while those around you are tense, upset, or irritated?

Perhaps the most powerful and positive background thought you could place in your mind is *relax under this pressure.* While the other person is boiling and fuming, adding fuel to the fire, it very well might be up to you to keep the channels of communication open. If you absorb the tension and frustrations of other people, no matter how overtly or how subtly they might be delivered, it merely means that your background thought is weak and tentative, ready to be assaulted and bruised.

Instead of meeting fire with fire, try placing a positive background thought in your mind. Say to yourself, in your own words of the moment, "I am going to relax my shoulders, my back, my neck, my eyebrows. This is only a signal for me to practice my great idea for the day." In other words, take a firm stand in your own mind and activate the principle that you know is true. Rather than giving the power of your thought away to this person — who may, in fact, want to intimidate and hurt you — take the power for yourself by keeping your thought where you prefer it to be. By this time, you know that relaxation is the key to the vault of riches and that those who are able to keep relaxed under pressure will receive thought about how to immediately and spontaneously solve the issue at hand. When you are relaxed, you keep your own intuitive and imaginative channels open. By relaxing your body and mind, you can always receive messages from the inspiration station within yourself.

By having your own relaxation planted firmly in the back of your mind, you will be able to say something or do something to cool off the pressure and help establish a channel of communication. Sometimes, you don't even have to say anything. Just by relaxing *consciously* when the pressure is on you, you will have a different perspective on the possibilities of the encounter. On one level, the person's anger could be very damaging and destructive. But on another level, you have the opportunity to rise above the attack by the power of your own thinking.

In fact, the best way to defend yourself is not to be defensive. The best way to deal with the situation is to maintain your own presence of mind. What the other person is saying and doing to you is happening outside of your own system, but what you are thinking is happening in you and will determine your own state of being. By reminding yourself to relax at precisely this moment, you elevate your own experience. You don't really change what is happening to you as much as you monitor the impact it has on you. You still can hear the words and observe the actions of the other person. You still can experience the wrath, but in a very positive and progressive way, you do not have to participate in it. You do not have to become a victim of this circumstance simply because you have a different background thought.

Although this is an extreme situation and illustration, the principle holds true even in circumstances of minor irritation and annoyance. When deadlines are closing in around you and a thousand things have to be done at once, check out your background thought. Try placing the thought of relaxation there. Remind yourself to take a moment to stretch out, to rub your forehead, to yawn, even to take a walk around the block to catch a glimpse of the sky.

Relaxing under pressure, even if it is only your background thought and not a physical action, will refresh, revitalize, and make you more receptive to those intuitive flashes of insight and genius. By maintaining your "cool," you can often lower the emotional temperature of the heated party. In this sense, being cool does not mean that you are distant, aloof, or pretending that what is happening is not really happening to you. In this sense, being cool means being elevated in thought, maintaining a clear level of vision within your own mind. By being cool, you will find yourself more receptive to finding a solution. It is very possible that this situation is happening to you for the purpose of maintaining your own cool and presence of mind. As you deal effectively with such pressure, you will train yourself to think quickly and progressively.

By defusing the heat in pressure situations, you will become known as one who reacts well to pressure. You will be seen as one who can communicate well under difficult conditions. You will then get opportunities to make big sales or play demanding roles — in which rewards are great and satisfaction is high. So, in every exciting way, your *task* is to keep your background thought clear and present. No matter what is happening around you or to you, the most important thing is what happens in you.

Relax under pressure — a great idea well within your grasp. Plant this background thought in your mind as a seed and watch the flowers bloom. They will come, in more shades, colors, shapes, and tones than you could ever imagine. You only have to nourish the seed in the fertile soil of your mind.

Listen Without Criticism

Have you ever tried communicating with someone who was not really listening to you? Remember trying to get through to someone who was thinking about what his or her response would be when you stopped speaking? Did you ever deal effectively with someone whose most important message was what he or she was *not saying?*

Communications is a two-way street. It is amazing how many people are *thinking* something other than what they are *saying*, and thereby miss important points coming from the outside because their background thinking is always in motion. With their internal organisms constantly in flutter, many persons cut themselves off from effective two-way exchanges simply because they do not know how to listen.

The most common complaint about poor managers or difficult bosses is that they do not know how to listen. While someone else is speaking, they are thinking about what to say next or looking for a way to punch holes in the message. On one level, they are going through the motions of communicating, but on that internal level of background thinking, they care only about their own, personal point of view. They are more interested in punching home their own ideas than in actually exchanging information and building positive relationships.

The best style of speaking *commands attention* and *invites participating.* When you create the conditions where the other party wants to offer his or her best and deepest material, you will soon have a meaningful, positive, and profitable channel of communication open to you. But you will rarely invite enthusiastic participating by the other in the exchange process if your background thought is one of criticism — of looking for the bad in what the other person is saying.

The original meaning of the word criticism was *"looking for the good."* The original critic was someone whose background thought was to help to make the exchange better. The best critic is one who can stimulate the audience to better achievement through a certain encouraging attitude. The most effective critics often make their points and help to initiate positive changes through support and praise, not through ranting and raving ultimatums.

When your own internal posture is one of tension, resistance, or resentment, you transmit a hostility, a superiority, and a self-righteousness that is extremely unattractive. You are setting yourself up for a fight when your background thought is negative. An unspoken battle rarely invites the participation of another. When you are mentally critical of another, only rarely will that other person want to work with you again.

In this light, one of the most important states of background thought to cultivate is *listening without criticism*. In practice, this means listening with an inner quiet. Instead of carrying on a running dialogue with yourself about what is happening or not happening to you at the moment, let your background thought be one of silent openness and receptivity.

This quiet background thought is the hallmark of an open mind. The more activity and internal dialogue are present, the more the mind becomes closed. If you look carefully, you will find that the open-minded person invariably is one who maintains a certain silence and quiet inside. The closed-minded, rigid person is always ready to throw out a negative comment or observation to anyone and everyone.

Therefore, a tremendously powerful and revealing background thought for the day is to *listen without criticism*. The exercise that has worked wonders for many people is to choose, at the beginning of the day, this background thought as their constant companion. Especially when dealing with some person whom you do not especially like or someone who has irritated you in the past, try making your background thought one of receptive silence.

See what happens when you listen with an inner quiet because chances are there will be a tremendous transformation in the receptivity level in those around you. When you yourself maintain an inner quiet and sense of genuine listening, other people will feel more free to talk with you, to be with you, to listen to you in return.

This is how your own personal background thought can

make a positive impact and effect on the outside audience just by its mere presence in your own mind. Although it is true that most of us have been taught to take mental potshots at other people while mouthing cliches and platitudes of pleasantry, it is also true that anybody can learn to maintain a background thought of quiet, calm, poise, and equanimity.

Yes, listening without criticism is not an easy thing to do, a goal you will not accomplish in one day or one week. It will take a certain persistence and perseverance to attain this quiet of mind. As with many people, you will probably have to set this idea as an intention every day for many days before it becomes rooted in the deeper, more creative levels of your mind.

But this one background thought will open your mind and leave you more *objective* and more willing to interact with others. By listening without criticism, you will receive more information to help you make a decision. The quiet background thought will more easily see the good in others and open doors to opportunities that the closed mind will pass over and never see.

By listening without criticism, you will increase your perception and your perspective. The greatest foes are of your own mental household. As you teach yourself how to listen quietly and positively, you will begin to see many benefits and rewards in self-expression. Rather than wondering about what you are *not* saying, people will like you and respect you for what you *are* saying. As you listen to them, they will listen to you.

More than that. Once you win respect for your calm, objective mind, others will seek you out for your opinion. When they come to you, your channels of communication will be wide open. At a certain point, available to you right now, all you have to do is listen carefully. You will get all the clues and details you need to raise your own performance one notch higher. A good, quiet listener can open doors that often remained locked to those who have something else going on inside their minds while others are speaking.

As you clear away the excess mental baggage, you can begin to travel lighter, see more, feel more, express more. The quiet background thought will be the means to refine your talents in the express business.

You have a way to practice this now. Write it down as an intention, remind yourself to keep an inner quiet as a background thought when you are dealing with negative people, and review your own state of mind at the end of the day. This mental housecleaning will take you a long way up the ladder of success.

Change the Negative to Positive

As you can tell by now, your background thought is a very private and personal affair. No matter where you are or what you are doing, you always have some thought in the back of your mind that is affecting how you speak, what you do, and how you feel. That little compartment of your mind is very much the control tower. From that vantage point, you will be better able to monitor, regulate, and control what happens to you if the primary quality of thought is positive during the entire day.

Quite unconsciously, many people carry a negative background thought with them most of the time. Negative thoughts are ones of rush, hurry, worry, inferiority, superiority, forceful power, and overriding lack. If you make a quick mental check on those people who live and work around you, you might find that many exist with a cloud of lack and limitation hanging over their heads.

Anytime you operate with a basic feeling or thought of lack — *not enough* time, money, energy, or creative ideas — you are operating your entire system in a negative way. If your basic pattern of thought is negative, resulting in an "I can't" consciousness, you will be working from a place of weakness and dealing yourself bad cards in the game of life.

If you feel you can't speak before a group or converse with someone in the company who makes a bundle of money and is in authority, your background thought will directly affect your behavior for the worse. If there is someone in your family or your work environment who turns you off and gets under your skin, you really have very little chance to make meaningful contact with that person.

In that case, try giving yourself a personal task and objective to change your background thought from negative to positive. In cases when someone is deliberately needling you or criticizing you unjustly, you have a tremendous opportunity to practice Multi-leveled (vertical) Thinking. While that person is targeting you for his or her own verbal abuse, keep your own background thought positive.

The major advantage of a positive background thought in this instance is that you can screen out the damaging impact of the other person's negative energy by the power of your own thought. A

normal reaction when finding yourself under attack might be to become defensive, hostile, and angry. You can get yourself heated up —
or you can climb the control tower and see the moment from a
slightly higher perspective.

Chances are that the person who is attacking you is in a
disturbed state of mind in his or her own consciousness. Very often,
when someone criticizes you, that person is really identifying something unfavorable about him- or herself. The overly critical person
is very unhappy with him- or herself and his or her own situation,
so why take those limitations as your criteria for behavior?

Just as the ringing telephone is a signal that someone is
trying to communicate with you, so anger, impatience, and criticism
are signals for you to rise above them in your own mind. In essence,
if you deeply desire to be a public speaker in any way, be it a good
manager, salesperson, or professional spokesperson, you will definitely encounter situations where others will single you out for their own
wrath and hostility.

You have an important choice to make. Either you accept
that negative energy and ingest it into your own system where it
begins to wreak havoc on your physical and mental health, or you
take a step up in your mind and exercise your power of control. If
nowhere else, you can change the negative to positive in your own
mind. You can practice the basic principles of mind control especially when the circumstances around you are negative. More important than what is happening around you or to you is what is happening in you.

Those who have practiced changing the negative to positive
as a background thought for the day report a magnificent change in
attitude. Attitude is to the human being what gasoline is to the car.
You may have an extremely expensive make of automobile, with all
the latest gadgets and trimmings, but without gas the car is going
nowhere. The same is true for the aspiring talented human being.
You may have all the college degrees and technical courses you
will ever need. You may own the finest clothes and have all the right
contacts. If you have, however, a negative background thought,
which is basically afraid, resentful, and suspicious of others, you are
going nowhere.

If you look for the bad in others and make an attempt to
cut them down to size for whatever reason, you are holding yourself
back. This is not to say that you have to like everyone around you or

agree with what they say. It does mean that you can mentally take the best and leave the rest. It means you can let go of your negative reaction to their negative input, which can only leave both of you negative.

Whenever you catch your background thought being negative, dominated by the "I can't" or "not enough" consciousness, take a step back and up in your own mind. Forgive this person his or her limited state of mind. Release that person from running around in your own soul with daggers and pitchforks. You can even bless the intruder, because when you bless and release the negative input of others, you are really doing yourself a big favor.

Even if you find changing the negative to positive in your own mind difficult during the day when you are in the heat of an antagonistic, frustrating battle, let go of the negative when you get home at night. If you have had an especially trying day and feel very worn out and exhausted, take a few minutes to realign your mind.

The traditional saying, "Never let the sun go down on your wrath," is a tremendously wise one. No matter what has happened to you during the day, make an effort to dissolve the residue before you turn off your lights. What you take with you into sleep will surely find a place in your heart.

You can soften and open your heart, or close and harden it. Once again, the choice is yours. The best speakers speak from the heart and in turn are heart-felt by their audiences. Your basic background thought for the day will always be translated and transmitted to your heart. You cannot entertain negative, critical thoughts about others without doing great harm to yourself. What you say about others you are really saying about yourself. If you consciously hold a positive background thought, you will better keep your balance. You will be more flexible, more mobile, more in tune with your potentials and possibilities. Fill your attitude tank with high test, premium fuel, and you will always be on the move.

Enjoy This Day

Over ten years of research has uncovered one basic fact about those people who had some degree of difficulty in speaking and expressing themselves under pressure. *They did not like themselves very much.* When it came to speaking and relating to other people in public, many of the participants in the training sessions had a low self-esteem. Their basic background thought was one of conflict with the self. On one hand, there was a deep need for self-expression, a desire to communicate with others. On the other hand, there was a basic thought pattern of fear, anxiety, and frustration.

When asked why this negative thought pattern existed and persisted, invariably seminar participants would cite one or two experiences in the past that left them feeling unworthy, incapable, and embarrassed. Somewhere in the distant past, a teacher, a parent, or a peer group friend ridiculed, criticized or maligned the person, leaving a strong negative impression imprinted on the psyche as a background thought. Having ingested, digested, and accepted that negative experience as "human nature" or "just the way I am," the participant would always demonstrate nervous mannerisms when asked to speak before other people. The mouth would go dry, palms would become sweaty, eyes would glaze with a strange glassy coating.

Very often, the crucial event had happened years ago, in childhood or during adolesence, yet the basic thought pattern lingered on and gained strength. Now, whenever the person had to speak and express him- or herself under the least sign of pressure, there would be a curious and obvious regression back in time to the psychological age of the traumatic event.

In these cases, the first order of business is to change the background thought pattern. It is always important for those who do not enjoy, welcome, and delight in the ability to speak to know that the background thought/picture *can be changed*. In the course of the seminar, it is possible to witness the change in the background thought and the resulting freedom and ease of the participants in communicating their deepest and "most secret" thoughts.

The pain that exists in many people stems from the conflict between what they really are — expressive, sensitive, gregarious individuals — and what they had been taught to be by their early experience. That one comment — "You're stupid" or "Shut up, jerkhead" or "You sure made an ass out of yourself" — had obscured a natural talent and capacity for free-flowing expression.

Like the old Street of Abundance in Pompeii, which had been covered up by layer upon layer of volcanic ash, background thoughts of past failure and embarrassment can cover up your natural ability to enjoy the common-union process. The conflict and pain one often feels when floundering under the spotlight of pressure always signify *a need and a desire to change the background thought*.

Because those reading this book may not have the benefit of the group support system that exists in a training seminar, it is important for you to get this one basic idea. Your background thought is very much like a record or tape that you play on your stereo system. If you do not like the tape or the song, you do not have to spend years and years in analysis to understand why you don't. If you do not like what is playing in the background, all you have to do is play another song. All you have to do is change the tape. All you really have to do is understand that the painful event in question is dead and past. You are giving it weight and life by holding on to it and playing it again and again, even though you do not like it.

If you experience pain, anxiety, or fear when having to speak in public, or to someone in authority in your company, or to a relative with whom you have had a difficult time, you can change your experience *now* by altering your background thought. You can give yourself another directive or thought. You can enjoy the experience, rather than fight it and withdraw from it. Once you change your tape, you can dance to a different sound in your own mind. If you go into the critical meeting or emotional encounter with the idea that you are going to *enjoy* expressing yourself no matter what else happens, the entire interchange will be different.

It is possible to arm yourself with a positive background thought each day. You can determine for yourself that you will enjoy all opportunities to communicate with others. Instead of living in a dead past or imaginary future, you can enjoy this day by setting *joy* as an *intention* at the beginning of each day.

In other words, play the music you want to play, a tune that gives you joy instead of reminding you of the limitations of the past. Let go of the event that happened and come out of the dark shadows. The truth of the matter is that you can let go any time you really want to. When you get sick and tired of repressing your every feeling and thought with the fear of what "might happen" or what they "could say," you can come out and come into yourself.

So a good personal task or background thought for the day is to enjoy the day as fully and as totally as possible. Don't wait for something out there to change before you enjoy your encounters. It really doesn't matter that your mother didn't love you or your father was supercritical of everything you did. It really doesn't matter that someday you will have another degree or a house by the water that will open the realm of happiness to you.

Forget *yesterday* and *someday* and go for your best *today*. This one idea — enjoy *this* day — has wiped out the negative background thought for thousands of people in the past. That fact only proves that every person is the master of his or her own mind, or could be. Your background thought of embarrassment or inadequacy is only a shell that is covering your true strength.

Do you really want to let others decide how you think and feel today? Do you want the insensitive creep from years ago to hold you back from what you do today? Do you really want to kvetch, moan, and groan about what they are doing to you today?

A winner is not one who never loses, but one who keeps a winning attitude after suffering a setback. The winning speaker or communicator is one who enjoys the opportunity to speak and communicate — even though the audience may not agree with his or her point of view. The act of expressing is what is enjoyable and satisfying. The *repression* of thought and feeling is what is painful and debilitating.

You can choose the background thought and feeling you have about speaking. If you do not like to speak to people, especially when you are under some kind of emotional pressure, you have a tremendous opportunity to grow through your barrier.

It is never too late to begin to change your background thought. It is never too late to learn new forms of background thinking or unlearn old ones. You can choose whether you have a growth complex or an inferiority complex. The nature of your own choice in this matter will be the author of everything that happens to you. Remember, *discipline is the commitment to a great idea* — an action you can take every day that no other person can stop you from taking. As you learn to say no to old habits and past appetites, you can overcome all feelings of limitation and frustration.

You already are what you want to be. Enjoy your opportunities on purpose. Set your background thought on joy, and you will marvel at the difference of the tone, mood, and feeling in everything that you do.

The more you think about it, the more examples you will be able to cite about the power of the background thinking in your own life. The thought pictures that you hold in the back of your mind affect everything that you do. Because these background thoughts are often unconscious or determined by a negative experience in the past, it is very important for you to take stock and identify what your current background thoughts about communicating really are.

You may take some comfort in knowing that most people have negative thoughts about speaking in public – and even in private. Many people do not express or articulate what is really on their minds or in their hearts even to those who love and care about them. Many people accept limited background thoughts from the past and play them out in their present life simply because they do not understand that it is possible to change them.

But you can change your background thinking by taking time each day to set your thought as you would set a stage for a play. The four background thoughts suggested in this chapter have worked for hundreds of people participating in the seminar situation. By no means are they the only good background thoughts for the day. But they are a start and they do point a dirction for you to follow.

At some point in your growth and development as a top professional communicator, you will have to determine your own background thought for yourself. One day, your task will be to determine your task. But for now, try choosing one of these four background thoughts and conduct an experiment for yourself. Take *one* thought and plant it in your consciousness like a seed. Remind yourself each day to nourish that seed and to pay attention to its growth.

If you were a gardener, you would not pull a seed out of the ground every morning to see how it is doing. You would give it time to root and grow strong by itself, having a certain faith and belief in the natural process of growth and development. You would observe and watch it, but you would also leave it alone.

In much the same way, think about your background thought in the morning and in the evening, then let it go. You do not have to hover over the seedling and watch its every move. Such a close, tense observance would frustrate you and might even retard the growth of the plant. Simply give yourself a few minutes to encourage yourself and firm up your background thought – then let the subconscious and superconscious planes of your mind do the rest.

Background thinking exists at level three of the Multileveled Thinking diagram. Once you are constantly in touch with that level by plugging into your highest circuit, you will find yourself being more in tune, in balance, on center. Like riding a bike, driving a car, or sailing a boat, it is awkward to do at first. But, once you get it, you will have that capacity at your beck and call forever.

Having a conscious background thought or "personal task" is a unique way of working for yourself and being your own boss, no matter who is signing your paycheck. Working with a conscious background thought is perhaps the best way of tapping your creative resources. It is most helpful when the pressure is the strongest.

Although there is a certain magic in the practice of a consciously chosen background thought, there is nothing magical about it. It is not something only a chosen few can summon up. Rather, it is a built-in capacity that everyone can use at any stage of life.

As you weave a great background thought into the fabric of your consciousness, you can have a positive experience independent of the circumstances around you. More than that, you will soon begin to see how a positive background thought for the day can actually shape and color the circumstances around you. When you practice presence of mind, you will gain a wider perspective on the whole of your affairs.

Promise.

5

Blueprints and Game Plans

In the hurry, scurry, and worry of daily life, we often lose sight of some of the principles for successful speaking, positive interpersonal exchanges, and satisfying living. We get so caught up in the deadlines and pressures of making a living that we often forget to make a life.

This "larger picture" concept is something absolutely vital to your effectiveness as a communicator. The basic problem is not your lack of talent, your lack of capacity, your lack of creativity. For many people, the most damaging obstacle is lack of training — a misunderstanding of the basic principles of how to communicate first with yourself.

To begin with, there is a need to understand and believe in the fundamental forces in the universe. Just as you believe that gravity will hold things in place or that electricity will light your lamp when the plug is in and the switch is on, you need to believe in your own ability to turn on your own light, no matter what is happening around you or to you.

In order to build your dream house, you first need a blueprint. In order to win the championship game, you need to execute a game plan. Blueprints and game plans first exist in your own mind as a thought, a concept, or a vision of how things *could* be. As you deliberately intend to use your past experience as motivation to expand rather than as reasons to limit, you will tune into a positive creative force within yourself. As you concentrate on the possibilities instead of the probabilities, you will clarify your vision and you will be much closer to successful execution.

Research shows that many people do not have a conscious blueprint or game plan when communicating or interfacing with others. More or less, they "wing it." They "take life as it comes." They react or counterattack the pressures and forces outside of themselves. In other words, they deliberately adopt a defensive posture. Caught up in the whirl of the game, we lose sight of how we are organizing and mobilizing our own particular and individual talents. We become so dazzled or intimidated by what is happening around us that we easily surrender the internal game plan, blaming other people for getting in our way.

Yet, no one gets in your way more than yourself. Over and over again, star athletes, artistic performers, and successful businesspeople confirm this one basic principle:

> *When you work with a conscious game plan*
> *and take care to execute that game plan,*
> *your talent will rise to the surface.*

When you think on several levels at the same time, you will increase your productivity and feel better about yourself. You will produce *more* with a higher quality when your vision is clear in your own mind.

Productivity is simply a function of having and executing a game plan.

For the purposes of effective speaking, both in a formal or an impromptu situation, the P.R.E.P. Formula is a game plan and blueprint for concise, precise, creative expression of yourself. If you keep the P.R.E.P. in mind as a background thought as you speak, your words will flow smoothly, logically, and precisely. You will have a line of thought that is easy to understand. You will display and radiate a definite *presence of mind.*

Even if the person with you does not agree with you, he or she will respect your precision of thought and your ability to express yourself with confidence and ease. You will be seen as someone who knows how to think and express under pressure. Once the other person realizes that you cannot and will not be intimidated, he or she will give you more of a chance to offer your own insights and visions of how things could be. Once you gain the person's respect, he or she will listen to your content in a more receptive frame of mind.

The P.R.E.P. Formula is a code word for *preparation*, the means by which you can always have something going for you from the inside. This formula will help you prepare for your scheduled meeting or examination or for your unexpected encounter because it is a *thinking process* that never fails. As soon as someone asks you a question or demands an answer, *think P.R.E.P.* By running your content through the P.R.E.P. Formula, you can begin to sift out the essential points from the nonessential. You can cut away the excess and get to the essence. You can picture your point of view for your audience and clarify what action you wish them to take when you yourself have applied the P.R.E.P. to your own thoughts. By speaking with this game plan in mind, you radiate a quality of expertise. You will know what you are doing above and beyond your words. This expert quality of thinking and speaking under pressure is what is known as *poise.*

Let's review the four elements of the P.R.E.P. Formula before we begin to practice.

P   =   Point of view

> *This is your* **overview** *on the subject. The P.O.V. is where you stand on the matter. In effect, it is the conclusion you have drawn from your study of the facts. It is a clear, simple, direct statement,* **often only one sentence in length.**

R = **Reasons why**

> *This element states the* **reasons why** *you hold your point of view. These reasons may be abstract, indicating your philosophy or set of values. They are an expression of the standard of thought that interpreted the facts.*

E = **Evidence, or examples to illustrate the P.O.V.**

> *Here you cite specific examples from "real" experience by naming names, giving dates, identifying situations that led you to draw your conclusion. Your evidence needs to be tangible data, something that exists as hard proof, which can be verified by anyone.*

P = **Point of view restated, leading to an ACTION**

> *To make yourself absolutely clear, restate your point of view, clearly defining the action you want your audience to take.* **Ask for a response.** *Specify the next step to be taken.*

A general rule of thumb to remember in the practice of the P.R.E.P. Formula is:

> *The first ten words are more important than the next ten thousand.*
>
> *The last thing said is the first thing remembered.*

That is why it is important to start with a clear point of view and end with the action desired. Everything in between will support your argument, but the greatest impact will be made in the opening and closing remarks. When those two elements are clear in your own mind, you will frame your presentation in the strongest, most positive manner.

The P.R.E.P. Formula is an organizing principle — a way to answer all questions and prepare your more formal presentations. For example, suppose you are a departmental manager who has to make an evaluation on the performance of an employee. The question is "Should Jack Johnson be promoted?"

P. = Point of view

Yes, he should.

R. = Reasons why

He works well under pressure. He assumes responsibility and likes challenges. He is a creative thinker, ready for the next level of productivity.

E. = Evidence, or example to illustrate

Last month, Jim Jones became sick near the end of the XYZ project. I called Jack Johnson, told him of the predicament, and he rallied. He came to the rescue by interpreting the data that Jim had gathered. He offered a solution that worked. Jack gets things done without complaining and is always willing to cooperate.

P. = Point of view restated, leading to an ACTION

So Jack is ready for advancement. He is a man on the move. If we don't promote him, we will lose him. He is ready now. We should be ready too.

As you can see, this is a strong endorsement of this employee. The speaker has no doubt where he or she stands on this matter. The P.R.E.P. Formula guides, shapes, and gives meaning to the words. There is a feeling that is communicated as well as the literal facts and words.

Notice that the longest section is the *E* or Evidence. This is the element most often left out of a presentation. When applying the P.R.E.P. Formula to your own material, be sure that you have clear, exact, and precise evidence. With good examples to illustrate, you can convince a doubter that your point of view is true. Without strong evidence, your point of view is merely an opinion, no better or worse than another person's opinion.

In our example to illustrate the P.R.E.P. Formula, the manager takes the opportunity to express himself as well as commenting on the business issue at stake. He leaves an impression about himself and his own strength in addition to the discussion of the matter at hand. Above the words is an attitude that then colors the words.

Long after we forget the specific words, we remember the *impression* that the speaker makes on us. We are left with an overwhelming sense of *yes.* If we want more evidence, we can ask for it, but the manager (in this case) has communicated a definite point of view as well as a sense of urgency, a feeling of action *now.*

Of course, the opposite point of view could be taken. The manager might very well recommend that Jack Johnson *not* be promoted — or even transferred or fired. The P.R.E.P. Formula holds true as the organizing principle independent of your personal overview. It simply focuses your thought in a logical form.

If you should read this answer in the example out loud, you will find that it takes no more than a minute or so to express. It is short, to the point. There is no excess verbiage. It opens the door for more detailed discussion if need be.

By taking this firm stand, the manager has offered a starting point. If he is respected, the action will be taken without further question. If there are other points of view to consider, this statement serves as a jumping-off point for discussion. It forms a foundation for commentary, and it *provides an immediate solution.*

The P.R.E.P. Formula holds true for both speaking and written communications. Once you have the formula working on your second level of mind, you will have something solid no matter what the question or issue at hand. You will have your own inner game plan working, which can be executed in many, varied ways.

Instead of reacting only to outside conditions and the pressures of the moment, you will have a definite thought force working for you inside. You have your game plan to fall back on, a blueprint for your own ideas, facts, and data. It will help you put things together spontaneously, saving you time, anxiety, and effort.

Your goal is to execute the P.R.E.P. With practice, this formula will help you think clearly and say what you mean. It will reduce the widespread problem of needless repetition and too many words. If you become known as someone who thinks clearly and precisely, people will know that everything you say *counts.*

However, you must also be prepared to act on your statement. You have to be prepared to back up your words with action. It is easy to say one thing and do another — so your credibility goes beyond the expression of the P.R.E.P. Words are hollow and empty if they are just words. What do you do about your words? That is what really counts.

In this light, all your words must be tied to an overall vision and positive set of values. Your goal needs to be a worthy one, which seeks to be of service to your company or community. Your depth and dimension of thought will make your words have great impact — especially if you do what you say you will do. The P.R.E.P. allows you to be more spontaneous because you have something working inside of you that is based on a specific, positive goal.

Knowing that you are *PREPared*, you can have confidence in your ability to think logically, calmly, and coolly under *all* conditions. You will not have to worry about how you are doing or what they are thinking about you. You can concentrate your thoughts on your own internal game plan, knowing where your strength really comes from. You can command attention by taking control of yourself. You can invite participation because you ask for a direct action or response from your audience. You can engage your audience because you are open to hear their point of view, initiating a feeling of common union. Because you know what you are doing within yourself, you can more easily relax under pressure, listen without criticism, change the negative to positive, and enjoy *this* encounter.

The P.R.E.P. Formula is like a communications insurance policy. It gives you something to fall back on, providing you with total coverage when everything is crumbling around you. It will come to your rescue instantly and immediately anytime you summon it.

But to receive the benefits, you must "ask." To weave it into your own psychological fabric, you will need to practice it and think in the form consciously and deliberately for a while. Just like a tennis player practicing a stroke until it comes naturally and "without thinking," you can help yourself by investing some practice time every day.

The more you practice with enthusiasm and energy, the better you will get. The more practice time you invest in yourself, the more evident will be your logical thinking during your business and social encounters. You can develop your ability to think on your feet by doing your homework on your seat.

The most fruitful means of practicing is by writing down answers to some stimulating questions in the P.R.E.P. Formula. Go to your blank book on a regular basis and practice the following efforts.

On the top of a blank page, write out one question. On the side of the page, write out the P.R.E.P. Formula, starting at the top and going down the page.

```
┌─────────────────────────────────┐
│         QUESTION                │
│                                 │
│   P                             │
│   R                             │
│   E                             │
│   P                             │
│                                 │
│         ACTION                  │
└─────────────────────────────────┘
```

Can you imagine a "magic lamp" inside of yourself — much like the genie in Aladdin's lamp — which can be turned on whenever you want? If so, you can get a feeling for what the P.R.E.P. Formula can do for you.

The following questions are extremely helpful. Answered in the P.R.E.P. form, they will help you embody this idea into your consciousness. As you ask yourself these questions and answer them to satisfy yourself, you will gain a clearer inside track on yourself. You will weave this organizing principle into your subconscious as a blueprint and game plan for creative thinking.

It is a good idea to answer *one* of these questions every evening. After you answer one of the suggested questions, create a question of your own and answer it in the P.R.E.P. Formula.

Take one full page in your book for each question. Give yourself some space and time to let the answer come to you. Don't force the answer into a quick mold. By giving yourself time to relax, the answers can come from the heart and soul rather than solely from the intellect. Let your answers be emotional as well as intellectual.

P.R.E.P. QUESTIONS

Did I have a good day or bad day today? _____

_____

_____

_____

What are my criteria for having a "good" day or a "bad" day? _____

_____

_____

_____

Of the four background thoughts presented in the last chapter, which could serve me best in my daily affairs? _____

_____

_____

_____

What does prosperity mean to me? _____

_____

_____

_____

Who is the most influential person in my life? _____

_____

_____

_____

Where do I want to be five years from today? _____

_____

_____

_____

What does success mean to me? _____

_____

_____

_____

What was my background thought for today? _____

_____

_____

_____

Whom do I admire most? _____

_____

_____

_____

If I could make one change in the running of my business life, what would it be? _____

_____

_____

_____

If I had to give my child **one** *piece of advice before he or she left for college, what would it be?* _____

_____

_____

_____

Did I think from the inside out today — or from the outside in? ____

_____

_____

_____

What situations make me worry, hurry, and scurry? _____

_____

_____

_____

What is happening in me when I am on top of the situation? _____

_____

_____

_____

My thoughts are creative. True or false? _____

_____

_____

_____

Am I creating up to my potential? _____

_____

_____

_____

Am I working toward a goal of self-development and growth? _____

_____

_____

_____

Am I investing time in my own bank of resources? _____

_____

_____

_____

Did I give my best today? _____

_____

_____

_____

Did I express what I felt when I felt it today? _____

_____

_____

_____

Which person turns me on the most? _____

_____

_____

_____

Which person turns me off the most? _____

_____

_____

_____

How do I feel about myself today? _____

_____

_____

_____

How do I want to be remembered? _____

_____

_____

_____

If I had millions of dollars and one year to live, what would I do? ___

_____

_____

_____

What is my visual picture of abundance? _____

_____

_____

_____

What is my greatest strength? _____

_____

_____

_____

What is my most unique talent? _____

_____

_____

_____

What makes me feel best about myself? _____

_____

_____

_____

I am as happy as I make my mind up to be. True or false? _____

_____

_____

_____

I know what I have been. But, in my heart of hearts, what could I be?

_____

_____

_____

What is the most important effort I could make to polish my speaking skills? _____

_____

_____

_____

Do I really want to get better in my communication exchanges? ____

_____

_____

_____

Am I willing to practice the principles on a regular basis? _____

_____

_____

_____

Am I able to let go of my fears and past limitations in expressing myself to those around me? _____

_____

_____

_____

Can I see myself thinking on my feet? _____

_____

_____

Do I believe I can develop my capacity for poise, relaxation, and concentration? _____

_____

_____

_____

Did I go through this day or **grow through** *this day?* _____

_____

_____

_____

Did I work at the **expense** *of myself or at the* **expanse** *of myself today?* _____

_____

_____

_____

Did I spend time **whining** *or invest time* **refining** *today?* _____

_____

_____

_____

What is my basic, core belief about myself? _____

_____

_____

_____

This line of questioning could go deeper and higher, opening dimensions and levels forever, so it is important for you to choose those that are most relevant to you and your immediate life situations. Each of these questions could be contemplated for many days, weeks or even months since they are designed for you to square yourself with yourself as the foundation for your activities in the marketplace.

Some people like to ask the same question of themselves over a period of time until they get an answer they can live with comfortably and consciously. When they write a new answer everyday and read their words out loud to themselves, they get a deeper sense of their own role in their personal growth and development.

The exercise is to answer the questions in the P.R.E.P. Formula consciously and deliberately so you can have it with you all the time as a background thought. Obviously, the P.R.E.P. method is not the only way to organize your thinking, but it is certainly one that works. You can save time and make discoveries about your own mind if you think in this way.

Be sure to emphasize the action you want to take based on your own answer to the question. What do you want *to do* as a result of your analysis?

Feel free to make up your own questions. The ones suggested here are meant to stimulate a positive line of thinking inside of you by giving you a format to follow. This is a guideline; what you put into it is entirely your own. The bottle gives a shape, but what is poured into it makes the final difference.

So sit back with your book and relax. As much as possible, shut out any distractions such as television, radio, telephone, and family or friends. Invest the time in yourself, telling those around you that you have to balance your account at the bank. For you do have a vault of riches inside of you. Your talent is inside, waiting to be used, polished, and refined to increase your productivity. It really does not matter what business, profession, or art field you are in. At some point, you will be asked to think on your feet and say what you mean. The sooner you take your own preparation into your own hands, the sooner that magnificent opportunity will come to you.

The P.R.E.P. Formula is more than money in the bank. It is another key to the vault of riches.

6

Nuts and Bolts— Comm-You-Nication

Good ideas are a dime a dozen.

The best laid plans ... often go astray.

"He did it once," said Charlie Dressen after a spectacular catch in centerfield by the young Willie Mays. "Let's see him do it again."

The "nuts and bolts" stage of Multileveled Thinking is where the action is. This is the very real, flesh-and-blood plane when you find yourself face-to-face with a difficult client, an irate colleague, or an unresponsive boss. The nuts and bolts of effective communication look and feel very different from all the abstract theories. When you have to make decisions on the spot and say the right thing under pressure, it is very tough to think on several levels at the same time.

If there is anything you learn after years of instructing others and participating in public speaking programs, it is that human beings are a very sensitive breed. The emotions, attitudes, fears, and fantasies of people come into play every day, especially when they are under severe pressure to produce and get things done on time, under budget, and with efficiency. Creativity and practicality are often two opposing concepts. Sometimes you cannot afford to take the time to be "creative." You've got to get your job done.

But this is exactly when Multileveled (vertical) Thinking can really work to your advantage. All you have to remember is one word — one word, that's all. It is simple, direct, profound. Remembering this one special, magic, wonderful word will lead to easy communication for you wherever you go.

The word is *you*. Y-O-U. A simple direct *you*.

Not yourself, your own job, your own set of needs. Not you the speaker, the actor, the one under pressure. Not you, the ego, who wants what you want when you want it. But you, the audience. You, the person out there, the one who is sharing the stage with "me" for an important reason.

All you really have to remember when speaking to someone else is that other person. To whom are you talking? What does he or she need or want? What is her purpose, his task? Where is your audience coming from? What can you give to them to help satisfy their set of needs?

Take the focus off yourself and put it on the person there with you. That is the best way to remove the pressure from yourself and clear the channels for communication. Whenever you feel angry, annoyed, or irritated, try thinking about the other person. Take a little step back and look at this person as if he or she had a message for you. See that person as a reflection of your own inner state of mind. Perhaps this person is there, bothering you and annoying you, only because you are botherable and annoyable. If you get bugged, maybe it means you are bugable. If irritated, irritable. If joyous, enjoyable. If loving, lovable. If communicating, communicable.

The remarkable discovery that many people make in this

study of multileveled communications is that all the psychological, grandiose theories don't count for much when the heat is on. When confronted with the real situation, people tend to forget what they are supposed to remember and fall back into old habits and patterns of reacting rather than thinking. They take care of Number One.

What they don't see so often is that they do play their part in the blockages of the channels. Because we as a people have been taught to be very critical of others and defensive of ourselves, we tend to see the other person as a threat to our own security. The people out there are often perceived to be threats. When someone says something to you out there that you don't like, it is easy to categorize that person as someone who wants to "get" you.

"Why is he (or she) doing this *to me?*"

That is one of the most common questions asked by people who have difficulty in expressing themselves either in public or in private. They see themselves as a target for the wrath of others, which in turn makes them get angry. There is a tremendous undercurrent of paranoia in many people when it comes to expressing their true feelings, attitudes, and ideas. That is the deepest, most important problem in effective communications — feelings of insecurity.

Many people are too concerned about themselves. Since they are so locked into the habit of judging, criticizing, and condemning others, they feel themselves to be judged, criticized, and condemned when in the spotlight. That is why so many people prefer to shut up, sit in the corner, not say anything, and swallow their feelings in critical, crucial situations when there needs to be communication, a common union.

Because of a basic sense of insecurity within themselves as individuals, people often just say *something.* The *effect* of the words is not considered — all that is important is that something is said, or something is not said.

The way to overcome this terribly self-limiting pattern is to pay genuine attention to the person with you. As soon as you give yourself the idea to think about the other, you take the pressure off yourself by giving yourself something to do. It doesn't matter who is right or who is wrong. It doesn't matter if the other person is a thoughtless, rambunctious jerk. What does it matter if the other person has real problems in expressing him or herself?

Why let the other's limitations be your criteria? Why reduce yourself because the other person cannot get his or her act together?

This is a very important insight if you aspire to be an excellent communicator. You have to be ready to talk to anybody and everybody all the time. You have to work to dissolve your feelings of prejudice, resentment, and resistance. You have to take the words *to me* out of your vocabulary. Instead of being so ready to ask why they are doing this "to me," be ready to assume that this person has appeared on your stage for one monumental reason — for you to make a positive contact.

In fact, it might just be that an annoying person has come to you for the precise reason of testing and challenging your power of choice. Either you give the other person the power to bring you up or take you down, or you exercise your own power of choice.

The most intriguing aspect of effective communications is that the more you think of the other person, the more that person will think of you. You can dissolve the tension by seeing from *the other's* point of view. Train yourself to *think of* the other person and you will always find a way to *communicate with* that person.

In face-to-face communications, either on a one-to-one basis or one in front of a group, *consider the other.* Your attitude toward the other person(s) is most important. Words will always communicate information. *Attitudes convey meaning.* Therefore, it is most important not to concentrate on the words but on what is *behind the words.* You can say all the right words and give all the necessary information, and still not communicate effectively!

Words themselves do not make an impact! The attitudes, feelings, and beliefs behind the words make the impact.

What are the attitudes behind your words? How do you see your audience? What effect are you having on them? Do they need or want to hear these words from you? Are they receptive or resistant? Is your audience important to you?

The subtle point here is that the *you* in comm-*you*-nication is a delicate merging and blending of the *you "in here"* with the *you* "out there." Every *you* — every person — in our society is bombarded by words and messages so that we are more reactive to your attitude than your words.

To communicate with impact, believably and humanly,

you need to be in touch with your inner set of attitudes *and* the needs of your audience. Your unspoken frame of mind will affect your audience more than you realize. Beyond your own feelings, you need to know as much as possible about your audience so that you can choose the right words and set the right tones. Do you speak with total concentration on your own message without regarding the other *YOU* in the picture?

In the nuts and bolts level of the communications exchange, *your audience comes first.* Nothing is more important than making them important.

But how do you do that? How do you turn yourself on to somebody you do not like, respect, or *want* to deal with? How do you prepare yourself for the freedom of expression?

The first step is to realize that most people get in their own way. The first need is to get a reading on your own level of resistance — your habitual state of mind and your unconscious patterns.

For example, make a list of the ten people in the world whom you dislike the most. Who turns you off? Who gets under your skin and makes you mumble under your breath? Who irritates you and *always* rubs you the wrong way? Who could you do without that seems always to pop up at the wrong moment? Who *really* bugs you? Write down the names of those people.

If you have more than ten entries on this list, don't stop until you have written all their names down on paper. Then step back and look at the list. Realize that your effectiveness as a communicator will be in inverse ratio to the length of your list. If you have a long list — perhaps including a whole race of people — you have a lot of work to do on yourself. Especially if you have trouble with women (if you are a man), blacks (if you are white), upper management, or cops, you are keeping yourself from the advantages of thinking on your feet. By harboring your own personal "enemies list" — consciously or unconsciously — you keep yourself out of the flow of the creative process. Your ability to communicate is as short as your list is long.

To show how this works, consider the following law from the world of physics, called Ohm's Law. It has vast implications and applications if we look at it in a human, psychological way. Suppose that every law of physical action has a mental or psychic correspondence; what applies to the physical universe also applies to the mental universe.

Ohm's Law states that current at the point of use is equal to the force at the source divided by the resistance in the channel through which it flows.

$$\frac{\text{current at point}}{\text{of use}} = \frac{\text{power source}}{\text{resistance}}$$

Applying this law to effective communications, we can see that your own effectiveness as a speaker is equal to your limitless potential for thoughts, feelings, and creative intuition, *divided by* your resistances of attitude, prejudice, and critical feelings.

$$\frac{\text{my level of excellence}}{\text{in communications}} = \frac{\text{my creative potential}}{\text{fears, resentments,}}$$
$$\text{prejudices}$$

communications, we can see that our own effectiveness as a speaker is equal to your limitless potential for thoughts, feelings, and creative intuition, *divided by* your resistances of attitude, prejudice, and critical feelings.

Think about this for a minute. If a person has a creative potential of 100 units and holds 10 units of fear or resentment, his or her level of expression is equal to 10. That person reduces by 10 the capacity to express if he or she holds those feelings inside. In other words, if you have 100 units of good feeling and 10 units of negative feeling, you operate only on the level of 10 units of negative thought. Amazing as it might seem, you level yourself off to the lowest common denominator of your negative feelings.

In a tremendously significant way, *as your level of resistance goes up, your level of productivity goes down.* When you have a high level of resistance in yourself toward any other person or audience, you will diminish your own ability to make positive contact with that audience.

From the point of view of producing and expressing your best self under pressure, you cannot afford negative attitudes, personal dislikes, or prejudices. *Your prejudices work against you.* No matter what "they" did to you in the past, you need to let them go to be free in the future. That's the *law*.

In the same light, when you relax your own mental resistances, you will find that "the current at the point of use" becomes more powerful and effective. This is why it has been said that your greatest enemies are those in your own household — your own mental household. Once you define *in yourself* someone as an "enemy" or someone you could "never" talk to openly, you succeed only in cutting yourself off from others as well.

Once the debris is in your system, *it's there!* The resentment you hold toward your "enemy" will also diminish your self-expression with someone you like. Emotional self-expression is very much like the physical digestive system. If your colon is clogged from years of eating poor food and improper elimination, you will have problems digesting, absorbing, and eliminating the good food you are eating today. Once that colon is clogged, it sends waste products of the body into the blood again. If you are holding resentments, pet peeves, grudges, or prejudices, you are clogging up your own psychic system, which prevents you from speaking with authority and thinking under pressure. You are doing "it" to yourself and then pointing a finger at the outside world for the limitations you are really setting around yourself.

Before you make a positive contact and connection with the prosperity and the opportunity "out there," you will need to dissolve those emotional blocks within you. There is no way to let the good flow in and through you if you are locking yourself up by keeping a long-standing enemy list.

In this light, it becomes of fundamental importance for you actively and consciously to dissolve the emotional weight you are carrying in you. It will do little good to try to change those people "out there." There is real growth possible if you begin to work to change yourself.

Go back and consider your enemy list. It doesn't really matter where those people are *physically* right now. What counts is that they have a life and a presence in your own circle of thoughts. They are living in your house. Your resentment is *your* resentment. You are carrying them inside of you as excess emotional baggage. You can shed this weight and slim down emotionally *by changing your visual picture of them!*

Take each name on your enemy list — perhaps one a day, like a vitamin pill — and spend some time alone with this person in the privacy of your mind. Visualize him or her in the environmental setting that sets off your "hot" button. See that person on the movie screen of your mind going about business as usual as if you were not present. Be a fly on the wall, a hidden camera behind the mirror, the invisible eye that sees everything but is never seen itself.

Is there anything you could possibly like about this person? Does he or she ever smile and laugh? Could this person ever fall in love or desire to make love? Could you ever see yourself shaking this person's hand and cooperating with him or her — just to prove a point to and for yourself? Can you change your mental picture of this person?

If you can, you can also let him or her go. You don't have to replay the emotional hurt surrounding this person if you don't want to. Since your mind is *your* mind, you have the power, the right, and the opportunity to screen any movie you like. Try putting a smile on the face of your "enemy." See this person as having something good inside. Change the way you see him or her, saying to yourself something like:

> *I release you from my mind, I don't want to carry you around with me anymore. I prefer to travel light. I'd like to extend and expand my circles of experience, so now I have to let you go. By letting you go, I am freeing myself.*

Don't underestimate this exercise or line of visual thinking. *You can change your relationship with other people simply by changing the way you see them.* They are not standing in your way. You are holding yourself back by holding them in. Change the mental picture; you will change the experience.

In past seminars, this has been an *extremely* important exercise for the participants, one that needed to be encouraged and supported for quite a long period of time. Even though people understand the exercise intellectually, it needs to work emotionally to be significant. As the participants took this exercise of dissolving their enemy list, they began to let go and release their own fears and anxieties about speaking their minds and their feelings under pressure. With the change from *repression* to *expression,* they experienced a tremendous transformation of attitude toward all their environment. As they themselves became lighter and forgiving, their environment became brighter and giving. Doors open outside with the freedom from inside.

If financial, emotional, and spiritual prosperity were available to you, *could* you get along with the number one enemy on your list? If your own happiness and enjoyment were at stake, could you change your mental, visual picture about your boss, your father, your sister, your fellow worker of a different color or social background?

Could you relax under pressure and think vertically? Could you give your best and keep the good within your enemy in mind — if it meant abundance and prosperity and opportunity for the rest of your life?

Make no mistake about it. That is what is in store for you if you take these exercises to heart and practice them as part of your daily routine and background thought. If you simply take a moment to see this irritating person as a challenge to your own creative, vertical thinking, you could plug into a circuit of energy and imagination that would raise you above every irritating characteristic that person has.

COMMUNICATION RULES OF THE ROAD

To help you get along with people you don't like and communicate with those who have given you trouble in the past, follow three simple rules. These are the "rules of the road" for communicating at the nuts and bolts level — where you find yourself most of the time. These efforts are practical because they are practice-able. In your office, at home, even in your car, you can polish and refine your ability to comm-you-nicate effectively by remembering three simple rules.

1. Relax Your Shoulders

When in the heat of battle, physically relax your shoulders, your eyebrows, your hands — any area of your body that becomes tense, tight, or taut. We have been speaking about the *idea* of relaxation to this point; now it is time to bring this idea into the physical realm.

Would you rather talk to someone who is open, relaxed, and receptive, or to someone who is angry, rushed, hurried, and hassled? Do you think and respond better when someone is waving a closed hand in your face, or when someone greets you with an open hand?

One way to tell how tense or relaxed you are is to notice your hands. Are they clenched or open? Mentally, are you a clenched fist or an open palm?

About five minutes before a big, potentially tense, possibly angry meeting, take that time to sit quietly and relax your body. Don't pace back and forth, going over the content that you want to get across. Sit back and relax your physical body — if you want to clear your head and be able to think on your feet.

A tight body inhibits creative, positive thought. Tension is the greatest constipator of talent known to humankind. You have the talent inside of you, but the problem becomes getting it out. There are more frustrated people at all levels of society simply because they do not know how to release their talent. Sitting on your talent is like sitting on a time bomb. Someday you are going to explode if it builds up inside of you long enough.

So, the trick is to *relax your shoulders*. Under pressure, *relax first*.

Set relaxation as part of your emotional game plan. Relax, if you want to be at your best.

2. Talk With, Not At, Your Audience

Have you ever been talked *to* in your life? Have you ever experienced someone making a special effort to talk with you? On the other hand, have you ever been talked *at*? Have you ever been the object of somebody's verbal abuse or attitude that he or she was better than you?

Of course, most people would rather be talked to and talked with than be talked at. Yet, many of those people talk at their audience and do not know they are doing it. In this light, it becomes very important to get a reading on your own style of speaking.

Do you talk to people, in the sense of *with*, or do you talk *at* them? What is your background thought when dealing with people at business, with friends or relatives? Do you see them as equals — people worthy of your words? Or do you see them as an obligation — someone to whom you *have* to talk? Do you feel you want to communicate — or do you feel you *ought* to?

If you feel you *ought to* communicate in any way, shape, or form, you will be talking *at* your audience. You will be talking at them, or over them, or down to them. Over and above your words, you will be communicating a sense of superiority or attack. You will not be inviting them to participate in the communications exchange.

Remember that communications is a two-way street. You need to be aware of the other person's inner state of mind and emotion in order to *choose* the proper tone and word. More important than what you are saying is what you are *not saying*.

The more you talk at people, the higher will be the wall you build around yourself. Get a reading on yourself in this area. Are you talking *to* or *at* people?

The more you are able to talk to and with people as if they are important to you, the more they will seek you out and want to work with you. You are more in control of your ability to communicate than you realize. Bring your audience into the picture. Be genuinely concerned with their needs, wants, desires, and feelings. If you care about others, you will play your part in building relationships that count and have clout.

A predominant figure in industry was once asked if he had a secret door to power. "Of course," he said. "I make it my business to get along with people. I know how to talk to everybody — from the president to the janitor. They all want to feel important."

3. Find Your Own Best Rhythm

When you rush yourself, you rush your talent. In the hundreds of seminars I have conducted, this is perhaps the phrase I have found myself using the most. Under pressure, the majority of people will speed up, talk fast, and focus in on the wall, the floor, or the ceiling. When the heat is on, many people confuse speed with agility. But the truth of the matter is that you will think and speak with authority when you maintain your own natural rhythm.

That raises the question of what is my "natural rhythm"?

Many participants have not identified the "original voice." Many men and women choose cliches — such as "super" or "cool" or "dynamite" — to express their feelings. They depend on catch words and phrases — and when they can't find the right word for the occasion, they speed up.

However, when under pressure, it is very important for you to slow down. By slow *down* we don't mean the actual rate of the words. By slow down, we mean to *take your own time*. Don't rush yourself. Identify your own natural way of speaking and don't allow outside circumstances to alter the way you speak.

Be sure you are consciously relaxing your shoulders while you speak. Go out of your way to talk with the person with you. Take the time to check yourself out. Are you really in a relaxed physical state, or are you going through the motions? Are you genuinely talking to your audience, or are you trying to get your point across?

When you rush yourself, you rush your talent.

More important than what happens around you or to you is what happens in you.

Determine to slow down and work in your own rhythm. You will find that you think quicker and on higher levels when you make it your business to slow down. You will get more done in a more enjoyable way when your intention is to slow down and think vertically.

You don't have to work harder. The trick is to work smarter. Keep the YOU conscious and active in the comm-*you*-nications process. That is really all you have to remember on this nuts and bolts level.

7

Fine Tuning— Reading Aloud

Tennis players may practice hundreds of serves a day from each side of the serving line. Golfers practice putts and wedge shots from all the most difficult positions possible to prepare for a big tournament. Pianists warm up with scales. Some race car drivers drive backwards around the track to sharpen their skills and fine tune their reactions to pressure.

What do stage, radio, and television professionals do to polish their speaking and delivery skills, to make their material come alive?

They read aloud.

Reading aloud is a practice technique to help put

emotion, feeling, attitude, and color into your words. On radio and television, announcers read scripts and commercials, but the good ones sound as if they are "just talking" to you. They have developed the ability to add something of their own personal feelings, attitudes, and rhythms to the copy, which gives the copy a dimension beyond the mere facts of the words.

Without emotion, feelings, and attitudes, any words you say will not have impact because they are not quite believable. That is why you can say all the right words and still not communicate effectively. Your audience has heard your words, but has reacted more to what was behind them.

Reading aloud is a way to practice filling in your words with meanings. It is one of those playful techniques where you can have fun and learn at the same time. It is something you can do for yourself and by yourself that does not cost a great deal of money, but it has a tremendous effect on your own inner life.

The simple act of reading aloud triggers a deeper part of yourself and awakens the built-in capacity you have for adding emotion, attitude, and rhythm to your words. Every time you read aloud, you strengthen yourself. Every time you yourself listen to how you sound, you can form a clearer picture of how others see and hear you.

One of the greatest problems in all kinds of public speaking and verbal communications is the monotone, the emotionless recitation of mere words and facts. The majority of people depend on their words to make their point. This leads to an overdependency on words and a frantic search to find the "right words" — the catch phrases, the slick slogans, the current jargon to make a point "get over" to the audience.

Very often, a salesman will fall into an unconscious rhythm where he says the same words in the same way all the time. Very often, office managers become known for their "buzz words," which become the office joke behind their backs. Like a mediocre, amateur actor, many people in authority positions believe that all they must do is mouth the words to have others respond favorably.

But just like an actor who is playing a role in a long-running show on Broadway, people in business need to find new ways to make their "script" fresh, alive, immediate. If it sounds like the same old stuff coming out of your mouth, the tired cliches and platitudes going round and round like a broken record, you will not make a positive impact on those around you.

In fact, once you earn the reputation of being a poor communicator, you will have a very difficult time getting other people to want to work for you or with you. You will meet constant resistance and resentment – just because you have not taken a good look at what you are saying or how you are saying it!

There is nothing worse than the canned speech – words said literally with no sense of your own individuality behind them. It is very important *to be yourself* whenever you speak so your own original, unique, personal rhythm becomes your trademark. Your speaking style can become your best calling card – that one trait people remember and like most about you.

There is no reason to imitate or try to copy someone else. Find your own rhythms and intonations that come out of your genuine emotion or feeling at the moment. Allow yourself to *feel* what you say. Turn on your emotional channels, and all your words will have depth.

Of course, the problem, as we have said earlier, is that most of us were taught *not to feel* – to suppress, to repress, and to box up our emotions deep within. We have swallowed our feelings to the point that we are often fearful of allowing others to experience what we feel. The rigid conditioning has made us less than we are and has turned many of us in against our own selves.

READING ALOUD EXERCISE

The act of reading aloud gives you the opportunity to feel. In this exercise, you are asked to *put emotion into your words* – just to let go and have an outlet for combining the intellectual with the emotional. The exercise consists of simply taking some printed material and reading it aloud for ten or fifteen minutes a day. You can choose any topic of interest to you. Some people might read something pertinent to their business. Others read biographies or histories. One famous acting teacher asks his students to read the history of the theatre aloud, to give them a sense of perspective on their art. You can read anything – articles from the magazine, the newspaper, passages from the Bible. Some read from the vast resource of popular self-help books, or books about personal growth and practical meta-physics. The sports pages are fun, but you will help yourself more if you choose challenging material.

The important thing to remember is that *what* you read aloud *counts. The spoken word has power!* The words and ideas that you speak aloud in a regular way have a tremendous impact on your psyche, so choose your material with care. Let your material help guide you to a positive point of view. Read about what you want to happen rather than what you don't want to happen. Let your material be an "upper" to give you reason to look forward with enthusiasm. Don't focus in on the latest robbery or rip-off scandal because you will incorporate that negative feeling into your own psychic system. You don't really need to register that emotion on your mind — at least not during these few minutes of reading aloud. And remember to *think as you read* — if you want to develop the capacity of thinking on your feet.

The exercise consists of reading your material *three times.*

1. Read the material through just for content. Get an idea of the message of the piece. Make sense of the words. Read each sentence until you know what it means *before* reading the next. Familiarize yourself with the content the first time through.

2. Add your own emotion and feeling to the words. What is your emotional point of view toward the content? Fill in the words with your attitudes, insights, feelings, and rhythms. Don't try to read the material "right" — read it your own way, putting as much of yourself as possible into the words.

The best way to make progress with this exercise is to read the material three times over three consecutive days. You might want to spend more time on any one phase, but the end goal is that you sound as if you are talking when you are really reading.

What matters is that you make intellectual and emotional sense of the material. You find your own connection into the words, then make them vital and real *for an audience.* Keep the other person in your mind's eye as you read so your words have a specific target. What effect do you want to have on your imaginary audience?

You don't have to agree with the content or like what

you read. What counts most is what you put into it — what you add of yourself to the script.

Reading aloud exercises are the "pushups" and "situps" for the excellent professional communicator. No matter what level you are on right now, you can get better by reading aloud. If you are just beginning, you can expect definite growth in confidence, poise, and style in about six months. Within six or eight weeks of practice, listen to yourfelf after speaking into a tape recorder. A small cassette recorder is a very valuable investment if you aspire to speak with confidence, poise, and impact.

This one exercise is really all you need to refine your speaking skills on your own. The more challenging the material, the more you can grow. The important thing is for you to hear yourself, to be yourself, to investigate your own emotional field. Take all different sorts of material to read, just to expand your own horizons.

Remember that the overdependency on mere words only serves to limit and confine your natural ability for self-expression. As you learn to trust your feelings and fill in your words — as you will by practicing this exercise — you will gain in confidence when you have to speak your mind under pressure.

It is great fun to read to a child. If you have a youngster in your immediate environment, read to him or her as phase three of the exercise. Take time with this person and you will make an impact that will last your whole life long. If your office or professional life is dull and boring, mechanical and routine in any way, read aloud. Be an actor for these few minutes a day.

This exercise is tremendous therapy as well as creative discipline. It's like soul food! The following four selections can be read in about ten minutes and are examples to illustrate the kind of material that has been helpful in the past. At some point, of course, it is best for you to choose or even write your own material. So, once you feel at home with the exercise of reading aloud to make your script come alive, try putting on paper some of your own basic ideas and principles of effective communication.

For instance, what are the most important lessons you have learned about life, love, or business? If you were a teacher, trainer, or parent, what tips could you offer to a young, aspiring, inexperienced person? What would you say to help motivate other people to think on their feet? How would you communicate to someone who is very resistant and resentful? What are your "rules of the road" for effective speaking?

Reading aloud will help you think on your feet, develop genuine poise, and express yourself spontaneously. It is your ticket to ride the highway.

The Rorschach of Life

Life is one great big Rorschach Test.

Every day we are bombarded with thousands upon thousands of images and impressions, words and messages, sights and sounds. There are so many different stimuli coming in on us all the time that each person must supply a meaning, a cohesiveness, a purpose, and a direction to all this noise and confusion.

The Rorschach itself is just an inkspot, stimulating my reaction. What is important is how I choose to deal with this impression on the outside from a set of principles from the inside. My reaction to any given moment or outside stimulation reveals where I am in my own consciousness. That in turn determines to a large degree what happens to me in daily life.

I either let the outside world control me and toss my emotional and psychic state of affairs, or I take command of it. That is what is at stake in the Rorschach of Life.

So, for example, in heavy midtown traffic, late for an important meeting, someone cuts in front of me, then stops. A garbage truck double parks and cuts off my lane. I now have the *choice* to honk my horn several times and scream "Meathead!" — or I can nudge my brake and ease around the obstacle while staying in the flow of the traffic.

The significant point for me here is that the beeping or the blasting of the horn — the "Meathead!" response — causes a negative input into *my* system. Who is the real *meathead*? When I choose to allow outside delays, disappointments, aggravations, and disillusionments to detour me and throw me off the track of my background thought for the day, I impede no one's progress but my own.

The "meathead" out there passes through my physical field in a couple of seconds, but my emotional reaction to that person stays with me and in me for hours, days, and possibly even years as a habit. The great danger is that my negative response will become an unconscious pattern of thought and feeling, an addiction that puts me at the mercy of every "meathead" in the outside world. The habit I pick up from "out there" becomes a dis-ease in my own system of thinking, leaving the "in here" a chaotic jumble of nerves looking for pills, booze, or cheap thrills as a temporary relief from all that seems to be coming down around me.

Of course, the choice is mine. Nobody is doing "it" to me. The garbage truck driver did not stop to pick *me* out as a target. He did not purposely make *me* his victim. I played the victim because I gave my power away. To avoid the toxins and poisons in my own body, I have to exercise my power of choice every day. I need to choose to relax my body when I feel any kind of pressure — especially because I have not done so consciously and deliberately in the past.

The truth is that I have to exercise my power of choice in the small moments of life to have that power active and accessible to me in larger, more important moments. Heavy traffic or annoying people are merely tests to exercise my power of choice. Those potential detours help keep me in shape, just as physical exercises keep my physical body in shape. It doesn't matter if it is sunny, windy, rainy, or snowy; I can exercise if I really want to. Nobody can do this for me. I need to do this for myself.

So, the opportunity is present right now for me to work from the inside out. I make decisions every day in many ways, so I want to choose my center and my core ideas very carefully. I want to have something positive, healthy, and progressive going on inside of me so I can rise above or go around any unexpected obstacles that suddenly dart in front of me while I am taking care of business.

I expect the unexpected, which helps me discipline myself and my thinking. I remember that discipline is the commitment to a great idea. To act on a great idea, I can help myself by giving myself a great idea to follow every day. The light inside of me has to be turned on by me. I am wired for electricity and light, but I often choose to remain in the dark of circumstance, economy, and sensation-seeking.

This is my house and I live in here. I want to keep it

clean, active, and functional by making intelligent choices in the fleeting moments of life. I can and will choose what level of consciousness I will operate from.

What images and impressions are moving me to action? What is the organizing principle behind my pattern of actions? What am I working toward? What do I really want to happen in my life? How will I choose to react to the next inkspot or meathead? Will I leave it up to chance, or exercise my choice?

Good food for thought . . . I am going to think before I speak.

Possibility Thinking

Something a colleague said last week struck a chord in me and set some wheels in motion. When I suggested that it was possible to keep a background thought conscious and active all day, from the time you get up in the morning to the time you fall asleep at night, he responded that it was impossible to have a "perfect day."

But what is a perfect day? Is such a thing really possible? Is a "perfect day" a great enough idea to go for all the way - to the nth degree?

To my mind, life is much more bearable and enjoyable when engaging in *possibility thinking* rather than *probability thinking*. Probability thinking is the usual brand of horizontal thinking. Probability thinking looks at the world of facts and figures, sees things as they are, then calculates certain odds and tries to play the winning side. Playing it safe means looking at the facts and statistics of the past as a significant clue to what can happen in the future. In the process, we become limited to what has happened in the past and thus confined to a horizontal plane of experience. We see things on the surface, as they are, and we tend to miss the depths or the heights to see things as they could be.

Possibility thinking, on the other hand, is vertical thinking. Possibility thinking discounts the odds, realizing that, in some instances, 999 failures do not count as much as the one success on trial 1,000. All of the great inventions of the past were a result of possibility thinking, as they were "never done before." For the great inventors and researchers, probability thinking was a barrier they had to overcome and set behind. Probability thinkers never break new ground; they simply retrace what has happened in the past.

The key feature of possibility thinking is the ability to let go of the past and get yourself out of the way of the present and the future. We discussed how the past encroaches on the present. The negative events of the past are part of the statistics. The mind, being magnetic as it is, will help create similar statistics if it dwells on those of the past.

In other words, don't think about and picture what you don't want to happen. What you fear comes true first. Especially in a catastrophic situation, it is important to think vertically instead of horizontally. When something bad happens on the outside, you have a choice. You can hit any button you want, but try to remember that the anger-rage-vengeance button sends toxics and poisons into your system. If you get mad, you may go mad. What has happened in the past is long gone, but your reaction is now and active. You can carry anger around with you for a long time if you allow yourself to, and in the process you are only damaging your own body and mind.

Now, I know this is not easy to practice and learn. Vertical or possibility thinking can not usually be internalized overnight. But in extreme cases, the law of attraction is at work even as it is in less extreme circumstances like frustration, delay, and disappointment. At some level, you are responsible for *all* that happens to you. Negative circumstances come into your life only when you cut yourself off from the creative flow of possibility thinking within you.

The picture I am trying to paint for you is that we live in a world of many dimensions. We live within a certain set of rules, laws, and principles, which only the possibility thinker can see with some clarity. The trick is to align yourself with the principles, which will then always work for you. If you wnt abundance, prosperity, and harmonious relationships, think in positive ways all the time. You must dissolve your fears, resolve your prejudices, and totally solve the emotional repressions of the past. When we can see the facts of life from a higher point of view, we are closer to the true potential within ourselves and closer to breaking original ground. In other words, we are nearer to big rewards, mainly because in our society the big rewards come from new, innovative ideas rather than old, stale ones.

When you can begin to think and see on several levels at the same time, you will find ideas and words *coming to you*. When you are practiced in this art of vertical thinking, you do not have to prepare your content. You have to study the content and visualize possibilities implied in it. Then, at the moment of pressure, you have to let go, trust the principles of relaxation, and let the words come to you. The idea is to stay free and open, not bound by past failures or insecurities. The way to turn on the big guns is essentially to leave yourself alone and trust the efforts totally and implicitly. Relaxation is the key to the vault of riches, if you only give yourself the chance.

The main point to come to terms with in this work is that we are training you to be leaders and original thinkers, not carbon copies of the past. You have the talent and potential in you to make key decisions and policies ten, fifteen and twenty years from now. But to do this, you have to practice twenty-first-century thinking. I am confident that people will be thinking vertically by the time 2000 rolls around, so you now have the choice and the possibility to be one of the early few.

This book is mainly designed to open possibilities for you. More important than what I say or do is what happens within you. My real role is to stimulate, challenge, and encourage you to go beyond all that you have done or attempted in the past. In some ways, I am asking you to relearn everything you have learned up to this point. You all have leadership and conceptual ability, but you all need practice time. Soon, the reading will be over and it will be up to you to continue writing in your book and visualizing yourself at the successful level you desire.

So, this time together is just the first phase of a great process. The qualifying test will be to what extent you can see ahead, to have the vision of the future that transcends the present facts. You have to see *more* than what is; you have to see what *could be*. In other words, change the negative to positive, and keep on top of the situation at all times. Think vertically from the time you get up to the time you go to sleep. Your goal almost has to be "to have a perfect day," or else you will soon be dragged down into resentments, resistances, critical harrangues.

The choice is always yours, and there are no excuses for not achieving what you desire. The important thing is to take quiet time for yourself every day, first to see yourself achieving your best self and then reviewing the day to see if you acted upon your great idea. Be still, be quiet, know that you always have an answer within you for every problem you face on the outside. That takes some faith and trust in the principles, but remember you have the choice to see from the horizontal level or from the vertical level.

I urge you to concentrate on what is possible rather than what is probable — on what could be rather than on what has been. Then, relax and enjoy the process. Count everything that happens to you as good, and you will be on your way to new vistas and new horizons. Get your lower self out of the way, and let the higher, intuitional self in you lead the way.

The best is yet to come.

The Law of Nonresistance

One of the most important keys to positive interpersonal relationships may be called the Law of Nonresistance. First of all, nonresistance is not to be confused with passive resistance, where you lie down and allow other people to roll over you, shrug your shoulders, and pray for divine justice. As with the other metaphysical "laws" of the universe, the Law of Nonresistance translates into a positive form of behavior and a powerful personal task for the day.

Nonresistance is an attitude toward others which recognizes that everyone who comes across your path is there for a reason — to teach you something about yourself and your talents. Because the psyche retains what it resists, any form of resistance to another person for whatever reason causes resentments, anxieties, and fears to blossom in your own psychic garden. When you dislike or criticize someone you only stir up something in your system that will bring you down, out of the creative, superconscious flow.

Whenever you meet outside stimuli with an inner curse of hate/hostility, you actually do harm to yourself. It is much better to relax and let go of your hostile reaction because you immediately lift yourself to a higher, vertical plane of thinking. It is especially true in business that if an employee dislikes a boss, the employee's performance suffers and he or she will do the job grudgingly. But having a grudge is a subtle form of having a crutch — it is an excuse why you cannot or should not live up to your best potential. The psychological fact is that when you dislike or criticize another person for some faulty character trait, you are actually identifying that fault in yourself.

So, whenever someone gets mad, blustery, or impatient, all he or she is really demonstrating is a lack of consciousness in and about him or herself. You yourself are often guilty of that which you accuse others of, so it is important to get a clear reading on your own dislikes. Who rubs you the wrong way? In any case of emotional upset, we often ask "What's the matter?" A more positive approach would be to ask "Who's the matter?"

This leads to the next major insight. Whenever something is the matter with you, something is the matter *in* you. Whenever you feel down, annoyed, frustrated, you have the power to push your relax button and take your mind out of the dark basement and put it "up on the twenty-eighth floor."

In fact, the more you can recognize your own prejudices, fears, and dislikes, the closer you are to harmonious relationships with others. The more you can put your own mental household in order by seeing through your anger and hostilities, the more comes to you in positive opportunity. That's the *law*.

Again, nonresistance does not mean that you have to agree with everything the person says or does to you. It does not mean you put away your own interests and swallow your own feelings. It does mean that when another person gets angry at you or puts you down, you see that it is the *other person's* problem. *That person* is out of control, at the mercy of the situation, and thinking horizontally. Nonresistance means that you raise your consciousness one notch higher. Turning the other cheek does not mean that you let the other person smash you on the left side after he or she has just finished smashing you on the right. It does mean that you tune into a higher plane of consciousness, so you do not allow yourself to be dragged down to the level that he or she is on. Nonresistance is one of the most practical and tangible forms of vertical thinking because we face so many situations and people out there that tend to cause us to become annoyed.

But why become annoyed? Why let the outside work in on you and eat away your talent and power to overcome? *Agree with your adversary quickly,* for the adversary is only in your mind. Your real adversary is *your own negative reaction* to what happens out there. You do have the power to choose your reactions to outside events, but you have to exercise the power and claim your rights.

Remember that you have a body, you are not your body. You have emotions, you are not emotional. You have a mind and you have thoughts, and just as you can direct your body to go somewhere, you can direct your emotions and your thoughts into a positive channel. You can do that any time you raise your consciousness to a vertical level, in about the same time as you can snap your fingers.

But you have to remind yourself of the basic efforts. Remember not to forget your inner power of choice. Remember to contemplate the facts of life from the highest point of view. Remember to relax and steer into the problem with the knowledge that the problem exists only for you to transcend it, overcome it, and grow toward a deeper realization of your own human, creative power. It really doesn't matter what happens out there — what matters is how you *react* to the *out there*.

So, say to yourself, as often as you have to:

I have the power of choice. I can react to the outside with an inner conviction that this is happening for the good, for me to learn how to take control of myself and my talents. I know that as I practice, I will feel better about myself and about my position in the company. I trust and have faith in my own inner potential. I know that there is something great and worthy I can do when I begin to exercise my own innate potential. Now I might be an acorn, but one day I will be an oak tree, planted firmly in the earth but reaching out and up to the skies. I am here to express good and to be a positive force and a support beam for those around me. I love my highest self and I will let my little light shine. I can do what I prefer to do, and I prefer to do my best and give my all. I will agree with my adversary quickly, for my greatest enemies are those of my own mental household. I am good, and today I will act like it.

There is much more to be said about the power generated and released by the practice of active nonresistance, but I challenge you to discover the depths of it by your conscious practice. You see, the fun of this is in the doing, not in the achieving. When you practice nonresistance, things will flow to you as you never dreamed before, but you will no longer be moved by things. You will be moved only by your own preferences, and you will see through quantity to quality.

You will become rich by the richness of your thoughts, and you will see that you can be happy anywhere at any time simply because you choose to be. *A man can be as happy as he makes up his mind to be,* said Lincoln. There are always thousands of reasons to be bitter and complain, but it takes the great person to rise above that horizontal level of being. The great person sees the wonder and the glory of it *all.* The great people give of themselves all the time, in all ways and always, because they know that life is for giving. Forgiving yourself and forgiving others (their limitations) opens a way for your own imprisoned splendor to come to expression. Practice nonresistance, not because they deserve it, but because you deserve it.

When you become an advocate of nonresistance, you will be in tune with everybody. You will be in touch with the earth and you will reach out and up for the stars. In some circles, nonresistance is the only way to fly, the only real way to climb the ladder to the heights of success.

What Station Are You Tuned In To?

As everyone who has a television or radio knows, there are many programs and channels available every day. Anytime you want to, all you have to do is tune in your favorite station and let the program beam into and through you. Especially when it comes to interpersonal and business affairs, one of the most important questions we can ask ourselves is "What station am I tuning in to today, right now?"

Are you most tuned in to the inflation station? The frustration station? The inspiration station?

The basic fact of life under consideration here is that what you think, you get. What you allow your mind to experience is then replayed in the circumstances of your life. What you tune into with the power of your thought, you replay in the affairs of your life.

In this light, it becomes crucial to keep your thoughts on *positive.* The more you criticize, complain, moan, and groan, the more you keep yourself out of the flow of good in your life. Because of the *magnetic power* of your thoughts, you actually create the conditions of your life by the quality of your thinking.

When your basic thought pattern is lack — lack of time, lack of experience, lack of energy — you paint everything around you with a dark, negative color. You then vibrate and radiate negativity, and you create false barriers, which then distance you from the good you desire.

Thoughts are like sunglasses. If you tint the glass a certain shade of red, pink, green, or blue, you color the entire environment with that shade of color. More important than the actual objects out there is the way you see them, and the way you see them is tremendously conditioned by how you think about them.

If you are in the habit of complaining about your boss, your job, your past, and your present, you are your own worst enemy. It is important to understand that whatever happens out there serves only as a stimulus to our own thinking, and we can think whatever we want to think. We make that choice all the time, either consciously or unconsciously. So why think negatively when you understand that your negative thoughts are an essential part of your problem?

Remember this one simple axiom:

> *If I am not part of the solution,*
> *I am part of the problem.*

A good way to keep your thoughts on the positive inspiration station is to measure your every word and act against this standard. Does this word and this act help in solving the problem, or are they adding to it? If there is someone I don't like who I feel is hurting me in some way, or interfering with my best, am I taking a step to solve the problem or am I adding fuel to it?

At the end of the day, you can evaluate your day by taking a step back, seeing yourself in various scenes, and asking — was I part of the solution or part of the problem? Anytime you find yourself resisting, resenting, or constantly challenging someone else, you are part of the problem. The major challenge of every and any business day is to meet the experiences out there with an inner game plan and intention.

Whatever station they are tuned in to out there — the hurry and worry station, the sensation station, the procrastination station, the limitation station — never has to determine your own choice or preference. Don't allow the limitations of other people to be your criteria for behavior. No matter what happens to you or around you, what counts most is what happens in you, so why not tune into the inspiration station all the time?

What does this inspiration station sound like? Where can I find it on my dial? Who is the sponsor, and how often does it broadcast?

First of all, the inspiration station sounds like nothing you have ever heard before because it plays only original music. There is no such thing as the top ten or oldies but goodies. The inspiration station is current, up-to-date, and completely contemporary because of the quality of its frequency. It is always new, always fresh, always up, always hopeful, pointing to new ways to solve old problems. The inspiration station features the sound of silence — the silence within that always provides entertainment, encouragement, and support for everyone who tunes in on a regular basis.

The way to find the inspiration station of your own transmitter-receiver is to be still, be quiet, take a moment before you speak and act in any given situation. The inspiration station is best heard in this area in the early morning, right after you wake up, and in the late evening, just before you turn off your light. All you have to do is stretch out, relax, perhaps yawn a few times to release all the tension you may have in your body and mind, and just be still. Some people say that the inspiration station comes in loud and clear if they breathe slowly and deeply, very consciously with rhythm, but others say all they have to do is turn within and seek a certain quiet of mind. They think no words about what they might have done during the day or should have completed. They make no mental pictures of things and people out there. Most importantly, there is no other radio or television program on in the background to interfere with the frequency they are trying to pick up. The dial is set on *quiet* and *listen*, and all you need is about five minutes worth to fill up your attitude tank for the entire day with positive, high test fuel.

But the truth is that the inspiration station is on all the time — twenty-four hours a day for you to tune in on your own private receiver. In fact, whenever you feel the heat, or the lack, or the pressure from things and people out there, remind yourself to tune in to the one frequency that will always provide you with poise, calm, and direction.

If ever you feel about to go out of control and curse, blame, or even physically hit somebody else, flick on the switch to your own built-in inspiration station. Take a breath, pause a moment, take a walk to the water cooler, or simply raise your thinking "to the twenty-eighth floor" (see p. 115), and you will find a way to be part of the solution rather than part of the problem.

There is no doubt, fear, or ill will being broadcast from the inspiration station, and there can be no doubt, fear, or bad "vibes" in you when you are listening to this inner sound of silence. When you are tuned in and on beam, you will radiate a certain light — usually called confidence, assurance, and poise. When you are on beam, you cannot be off target — and the trick is to practice the presence of this high-level, high-powered frequency.

All you really have to do is to know that it's there, sponsored by the same infinite intelligence that created you and the world in the first place. Once you begin to envision God as a special presence or capacity for vertical thinking within yourself, once you see the principle governing all physical action, you can begin to meet and rise above any thorny issues and problems you may be faced with on the job, with friends, families, or lovers.

Once you begin to practice the presence of mind given to you at birth by virtue of your humanity, you will uncover and release a tremendous power, which is now dormant inside you. When you become a constant listener to the inspiration station, you will be sure that no matter what happens to you or around you, the most important thing is what happens in you.

The inspiration station will lead you to sing your own song, dance your own dance, smile your own smile, and be your own self. You are an original. There is nobody else like you, and to really take advantage of your own special gift, you only have to tune in to the right station. The more you can quiet your own thoughts, fears, doubts, and suspicions, the more will be revealed to you from the higher realms of imagination, intuition, and inspiration.

There is nothing more powerful than an inspired idea whose time has come. There is no more joyous or fulfilling way to work than under the guiding force of inspiration. When the spirit moves you, creative ideas will flow and the resources will appear for you to bring your idea into being.

That's the law. You only have to cooperate. You only have to tune in. You only have to be conscious of what is really there and who you really are. Success, prosperity, happiness, and fulfillment are right here for the taking — every day in every way. So choose this day what station you listen to.

What kind of programming do you prefer? You are the director and you are the arranger. The choice is always up to you.

The best material for the reading aloud exercise is what helps you to clarify and identify your basic point of view for the day. Choose material that you can enjoy and have a good time with, even something from childhood such as *Alice in Wonderland*. Many people have felt a certain kind of freedom in reading poetry or children's stories. The most important point is that you begin to think as you read, practice articulating words and feelings together, and reach for colorful expression of attitudes above and beyond the literal words.

Discover the many dimensions of this exercise for yourself. Hear yourself grow. That's the fun of it all.

8

Favorite Stories

Everyone has a story to tell. There is something very special and extremely attractive about someone who knows how to tell a good story — especially one that makes a point in a visual, dramatic, vivid way.

One distinguishing feature about excellent speakers is that they have a vast repertoire of good "inside" stories. Depending on the needs, wants, and desires of their particular audience, they have a story that seems to hit home. A good story can make a point gently, with a distance, with a detachment that does not hit the audience over the head. A good story is often offered with the feeling of "If the shoe fits, wear it." The story does not tell people *what* to do. It points out "how to" do it. Besides, children of all ages love a good story.

One of the most delightful and intriguing exercises that helps form a solid foundation for your own ease, grace, and style is to collect your own favorite stories. No matter whether it is a formal, informal, impromptu, or social occasion, storytelling is perhaps the most memorable manner of presenting your point of view to make a lasting impact. A good story combines all the elements of the P.R.E.P. Formula, wrapping the package in a human, realistic, identifiable way.

For example, think of the fables of Aesop. They have a practical as well as a philosophical dimension. His stories solve an immediate problem, but they also give direction for future behavior. The fable, in this case, puts some distance and perspective on the immediate moment, breaking tension or a stalemate by lifting the entire drama into a different dimension.

It really doesn't matter what business or profession you are in. Every line of endeavor has its own "classic" stories — ones that educate as well as entertain, ones that can be kept in mind under pressure to help you guide and polish your own style of speaking.

Go on a "story hunt." Look for stories that appeal to you and fire your thinking and imagination. Keep an eye open for scenes that have a special meaning, scenes that reveal human nature or the way the world works. Jot down these stories in your private journal and tell them to yourself. You could certainly tell a story as part of your *reading aloud* exercise.

Storytelling can sharpen your eye *and* refine your listening skills. As you begin to write and tell your own stories, you almost automatically develop your capacity for hearing the points of view of other people. As you discover the principles of good storytelling for yourself, you have another standard for judging the words of other people.

The stories you write yourself and tell in your own personal, individual manner can become your trademark, which distinguishes you from everybody else. Stories are especially good vehicles for breaking the ice at a business luncheon, a formal meeting, or social gathering. One always admires someone who can tell a story that captivates the imagination.

What ten stories have stayed with you the longest? What are the moments that have made the greatest impression on your life? Do you know the story of anyone who has succeeded or failed because they obeyed or misunderstood some of the basic principles of prosperous living? What stories have "sold" you on some idea, product, or person in the past?

We are often told that one picture is worth a thousand words. A good story is worth its weight in gold. One story that interprets and focuses all the facts can make more impact than one hundred pages of statistics.

There are several elements of good storytelling.

1. Set the story in a specific time, place, and situation. Have your characters want something specific. Let the conflict develop out of different goals or objectives.

2. Have something happen in your story. The conditions should be different at the end than in the beginning.

3. Have the main character learn or see something in the unfolding of the events.

4. Make your words visual — help your audience create a visual picture for themselves where they can "see" what is going on.

5. The first ten words are worth the next ten thousand. The last thing said is the first thing remembered.

As with all "rules of the road" or techniques for success, these five steps are not rigid or definite. They are simply points to be considered when delivering your own material. You do not have to use all of them or any of them — just see how they can help you make your material come alive.

So, begin to gather your own treasure of stories. Constantly add to your repertoire, making adjustments and amendments as you yourself grow and expand into an ever larger circle. Make your storytelling fun and satisfying for yourself. When you have a good time, you will invite your audience to enjoy themselves with you. All of you can enjoy the experience and have a good time in the exchange.

A SAMPLE STORY COLLECTION

Here are some favorite stories I have collected over the years, which I invite you to add to your repertoire. Some are vignettes I have heard other people tell. Some are original. What is most important is that you make these stories your own. Tell them in *your* way. Make them real and emotional for yourself. Have them come alive through your own camera lens.

Read the stories aloud, then talk them into a tape recorder. Tell them until they sound right to you, the listener who has never heard this person on the tape before. Play with this favorite story exercise — the playfulness is the magic.

Sit on Your Egg

Once I used to think that chickens were very dumb birds, clucking, scratching, and cockle-doodle-doing their way around the barnyard all day long. They would peck and scratch, chase each other around over a kernel of corn, ruffling their feathers while waddling in the confines of their wired-in fence. They would spend the whole day in meaningless cackle, never really accomplishing anything.

But then I began to get a feeling for an egg. The hen, when creating new life, will leave the cackling and scratching of the barnyard, will go off in the quiet, and just sit awhile. She will cradle that little egg, keeping it warm and nestled close to her until, twenty-one days later, a new creature will begin to peck its way through the shell.

For exactly twenty-one days, that dumb old hen will withdraw and just sit on the little egg until it hatches. Perhaps she'll go out into the barnyard once in a while to scratch, claw, and cluck with the other hens. Perhaps she'll peck around for a few grains of food and get a drink of water. Perhaps she will prance and dance her way around the strutting rooster for a few moments, but invariably she will go back to the calm and quiet of her great idea.

She will treat that egg with unaccustomed respect and reverence because she instinctively knows that she must play this quiet role in delivering new life.

When was the last time you sat quietly and warmly for twenty-one days? Have you ever paid calm and quiet attention to an original impulse, knowing that it was going to take at least three weeks before coming to the light of life?

We are all hens, or we could be. It does take some calm, quiet, confident sitting on the "egg" before the idea takes flesh and blood.

All around they cluck and crow
but only in calm and quiet can the idea grow.

The Uphill Battle

Did you ever feel as if you were pushing a boulder up a mountain? Ever think you really don't want to go on or continue your quest for success? Did you ever think that all those people out there don't recognize you or appreciate your talents?

Consider the facts of life of this pioneer, one who persevered above and beyond the call of duty.

Incident	Age
Failed in business.	22
Ran for legislature, defeated.	23
Failed in business, again.	24
Elected to legislature.	25
Sweetheart died.	26
Suffered nervous breakdown.	27
Defeated for speaker of legislature.	29
Defeated for elector.	31
Defeated for Congress.	34
Elected to Congress.	37
Defeated for Congress.	39
Defeated for Senate.	46
Defeated for Vice-President.	47
Defeated for Senate.	49
Elected President of the United States.	51

That's the resume of Abraham Lincoln.

The Worry Button

Once the founder and president of a thriving American corporation was asked the secret of his success.

"My worry button," he replied, pointing to a simple, doorbell contraption on his desk. "When I first came to this office thirty years ago, I set this bell on my desk and called it my worry button. Anytime I wanted to worry or agonize over anything to make the situation worse, I promised myself I would first have to push my worry button. Then I could get all my thoughts scrambled and my blood hot and truly be in deep water.

"The secret of my success is that in thirty years, I never pushed this button once."

Five Hours a Day

A young reporter was assigned to interview Pablo Casals, the world famous cellist, on his ninetieth birthday. The eager cub, anxious to make a good impression, went to Casals' home a few hours before the appointed interview time to try to get a better visual picture about the grand master.

Five hours later, he was still sitting in the waiting room while the beautiful sounds of the musician's cello came drifting through the room. When Casals came out of his inner chamber, the young man said "Why, I've been waiting for five hours. What were you doing all this time?"

"Practicing," said Casals with a contented sigh.

"Practicing?" said the reporter incredulously. "You are the best, most respected cellist in the world. Why do you have to practice five hours a day?"

"Simple," replied the master with a smile. "I want to get better."

Po(i)se

The difference between *pose* and *poise* is one letter — a simple *i*. Without that *i* in the picture, all you can do is pose. To acquire true poise and transcend all poses, simply add your own *I*. Allow the originality of yourself to come through, and you will always have poise.

What is the definition of poise? Broken down letter by letter, poise means the recognition of the:

P	=	**possibility and power**
O	=	**of**
I	=	**instantaneous**
S	=	**self**
E	=	**expression**

Poise is the recognition of the possibility and power of instantaneous self–expression. Keeping that possibility in mind under all circumstances, you will always display poise. It's when you feel you can't express your true self that you are getting into trouble. To get beyond a "pose," you have to add an "*I*" — your eye, your sensitivity, your best self.

Check Your Baggage

Once upon a time, holy men were required to take strict vows that were intended to put them on the "highway to revelation." Two young priests were ordained together, then spent the next ten years in quiet meditation and prayer in a remote monastery. They had vowed never even to think of carnal pleasures or envision a woman's body, much less ever touch female skin.

When the time came to leave the holy monastery, the two priestly companions were sent to the same distant province to practice their faith. As they walked along the road on a dark and stormy night, they found themselves at the shores of a raging river.

There, stranded on the bank, was a beautiful woman in distress, in danger of being swallowed up by the rising waters.

"Please help me across the river," she pleaded.

One priest turned away, driven by his solemn vow never to contact the flesh of a woman. The other promptly picked her up, carried her safely across the river, set her down on the far bank, and then rejoined the other priest.

"How could you do that?" angrily demanded his companion. For twenty miles, the rebuke continued. "Vows were broken . . . the law was trespassed . . . a cardinal principle ignored . . . a great sin committed at the first moment of temptation . . . ."

Finally, the priest who had "transgressed" had enough. He stopped and turned toward his complaining companion. "Look, I picked up the woman, carried her away from danger, set her down, and let her go on her way. You have been carrying her for twenty miles. Her weight is on you, not me."

How many incidents from the past have you been carrying for "twenty miles"? The incident is dead and gone. Does it still have life in your own mind and heart? If so, let it go.

The highway is only for those who can relax, let go, forgive, and travel light. Those who carry the weight of the past on their shoulders are soon left far behind.

The Lucky Bill

A young soldier was discharged from the army after World War II with a fire of ambition burning in his soul. He was enthused by the opportunities and possibilities stretching before him in his active imagination.

He joined a corporation that promised good pension plans, health benefits, and economic security — but three years later, he found himself going in circles, caught in a depressing holding pattern. No one around him seemed to appreciate his enthusiasm. No one took to his suggestions or his aggressive talents. Not one of the promotions ever promised panned out. He was bitter, angry, and on the outside looking in.

One afternoon, he decided to quit. He was ready to leave, pull up stakes, and head for the promise of California. But on that very day, while walking to his tenement home, he spied a green object in the gutter of the busy Manhattan street. He picked it up, and to his complete shock, he saw that it was a $1,000 bill!

Now, in the late 1940s, $1,000 meant a lot more than it does today. For $1,000, the young man could live reasonably, paying basic rent, food, and clothes for quite some time.

The young man ran home, ecstatic and joyous about his "good luck." He was glowing and happy. He spent the entire evening dreaming about what he would do with this unexpected gift. He stared at it and fondled it, kissing it like a baby. He tucked it in his drawer, taking it out now and then to look at it and make sure. He couldn't quite believe his good fortune.

With his secret money, he went back to his job with an entirely different attitude. It didn't matter what his boss said or didn't say to him. He had his insurance policy, and he could leisurely look around for something else. He was all smiles, pleasant to everybody. He was willing to do anything because he had some cash in the bank, giving him the mental freedom to come and go as he pleased.

Naturally, this new attitude was noticed immediately. His boss marveled at this ball of fire. He wondered if he had overlooked something in the young veteran. The promotion came soon after. Within a month, the young man was one of the top salesmen in the company. He was offered a territory all his own in a new section of the country, with untapped possibilities for growth.

Now it was time to break down his secret prize into smaller bills. So, he went to the bank and slid the $1,000 under the cashier's window. The teller looked at the bill, looked up at him, then back down at the bill.

"Excuse me, sir," the teller said quietly. "Where did you get this bill?"

"You won't believe me," replied the young man, "but I found it in the street."

"I'm afraid you'll have to come with me to the manager's office. This bill is counterfeit."

But the young man's raise, his promotion, and his new territory were not counterfeit. He had assumed the $1,000 to be real in his own mind and had acted *as if* he had money in a special account. His actions and attitudes followed that background thought.

The bill itself was worth nothing. The meaning he gave it was everything.

So, act as if you believe something is true even before it is. You will be sure to help bring this desired condition into your life — mainly by your attitude.

Seeing From the Twenty-eighth Floor

Have you ever seen the world from the twenty-eighth floor? Have you ever had the chance to look out over the city and the countryside from that high point of view?

The manager of the most efficient, harmonious, and good-spirited department of a modern, international corporation was asked why the morale of his people was so high. "I take each employee on the superdeluxe twenty-eighth floor tour," he responded cheerfully.

It seems that every time someone was assigned a position in his department, the manager took this person down to the basement where everything was dark and damp, covered with dust, with no natural light seeping through at all.

"How do you feel down here?" the manager asked.

"Like I want to get out. It's depressing — even a bit scary."

"That's basement thinking," the manager said.

Then they went up to the lobby floor. There was always a flurry of activity, with people revolving around the doors in a hurry.

"How do you feel here?"

"Better, but confused. I don't know exactly where I'm supposed to go or what I am supposed to do."

"That's first floor thinking."

Then the manager took the new employee up to the third floor where there was a little balcony that overlooked the street and out at the other office buildings.

"What's your reaction to this?" the manager asked pleasantly.

"I can see a little more, but it's still pretty shadowy."

"Third floor thinking."

Then they went up to the twenty-eighth floor and looked out over the whole panorama.

"How would you like a career up here?" the manager asked.

"I like it. I can see far and wide. There's light and space and room to breathe. I can see the patterns down below."

"That's thinking from the twenty-eighth floor."

"So what?" was the typical reaction.

"Close your eyes," instructed the manager. "See yourself in the basement again." The new employee went back to the basement in his mind. The manager snapped his fingers.

"Now see yourself in the lobby." The employee changed the picture on his mental movie screen. The manager snapped his fingers again. "Now see yourself on the third floor balcony." Fingers snapped. "Now see yourself on the twenty-eight floor." The mental picture changed, and the new employee invariably smiled.

"Around here," the manager suggested, "we see all problems 'from the twenty-eighth floor.' If you ever find yourself thinking as if you were trapped in the basement, snap your fingers and go up to the twenty-eighth floor in your mind. Just snap your fingers — it's an instantaneous reminder to see from a higher point of view, and it's a call for help at the same time. If you ever snap your fingers three times in one day, come to my office. A three-snap problem is one I should know about right away!"

The Mental Decongestant Laxative

Wouldn't it be great if there were a product on the market for mental congestion and constipation? Can you imagine the tremendous sales potential if people could buy a pill and flush out all the waste fears, worries, doubts, anxieties, resentments, and resistances that clog up the mind, sometimes for years?

It's very possible to have chronic mental constipation. The overstuffed mind adds weight just as the overstuffed stomach does. The stuffy mind is just as bad as a stuffy nose.

The remedy could be presented as a super laxative pill, in many colors and flavors. We could plug it in thirty-seconds or sixty-seconds spots. "Take this fresh-tasting tablet and clean out your mental intestines. Eliminate, circulate, evacuate. A clean mind for a clean life. Keep your head as clean as your kitchen. Zaaam!"

Is there a way we can manufacture, market, and promote a mental decongestant laxative for the consumer market?

Tom Seaver's Credo

In a 1970s National League Playoff game between the two contending teams for the pennant, Tom Seaver, the outstanding pitcher for a team not involved in the playoffs, was the color commentator. He was hired as an announcer because he brought a keen eye to the events on the field, because he knew the inside stories of the players, and because he spoke the language of the dugout.

The game was close, with the score tied 1-1 in the bottom of the seventh inning. The first batter bunted the ball down the third base line. The pitcher fielded the perfect bunt, rushed, and threw the ball over the first baseman's head trying to get the fleet runner out.

With a man on first and nobody out, you have a classic sacrifice situation. The next batter squared away and bunted the ball down the third base line to advance the runner into scoring position at second base. The pitcher, still nervous and rushed, scooped up the ball, saw that he had no play at second, pivoted, and again threw the ball wild at first base.

Now there were runners on first and second, and nobody out — a dangerous situation. Seaver broke the tension in the press box with his giggly laugh. His comment was, "It looks like they're going to do it until they get it right."

Sometimes a person will ask how long one should stick with a particular background thought. One day? Two days? Ten days? Two months? Do it until you get it right.

Am I My Resume?

One of the most striking, effective numbers in the hit Broadway musical *A Chorus Line* is the song, "Am I My Resume?" A young actress looks over her resume that she must give to the director at the audition and asks herself if that is really what she is — her resume?

Somewhat wistfully, she tries to explain that there is more to her than is contained on that piece of paper listing where she has been, what she has done, where she has studied. The essential part of her has not been captured by that piece of paper with all the facts of her life, yet that resume seems to be what is important to the world outside.

At some point in our professional careers, we are usually asked to write a resume to give a picture of our qualifications for a certain job. We list the important dates and places, but do we include a picture of where we want to go? Do we include a picture of what our strengths are? Do we dare to put down our vision of what we could be and where we see ourselves at our best?

You probably have written a job resume, but what about a life resume? As if you were looking back over your whole life, what have you accomplished that is beyond the facts? What have you overcome? What can you see yourself doing if you were working at your optimum level?

A good resume always looks for the *could be*. Many employers would welcome a statement of purpose that articulates unseen qualities as well as literal facts. Try keeping your life resume up-to-date by looking into the future.

Write your life resume as if you were five years older. What has happened in these *past* five years? The five years just ahead of you?

Look back on your goal. See it as already in progress. Fill in your resume with all the information that can have you say "This is what I am. I am my resume and more!"

Mentally Tough

Are you mentally tough?

In these days of positive thinking and popular self-help books, one of the desired goals is to train yourself to be *mentally tough*. In professional sports, in sales training seminars, in the routines of business life, we are told that mental toughness is something that can carry us over all nagging obstacles. We are urged to "hang tough," to "tough it out," to remember "when the going gets tough, the tough get going." Although there is a grain of truth to these cliches, there is often an underlying danger that harms as many people as it helps.

It all depends on what you mean by *tough*.

Some people think that mentally tough means to be a hard-headed ramrod. Some think that you are mentally tough when you run roughshod over people to take care of number one, "winning" your point of view whatever the psychological and emotional costs to everyone concerned. When tough means *you do it my way or else,* tough is rough.

When tough has as its underlying meaning "will-ful-ness," the person is setting him or herself up for a great downfall. The willful person becomes a target for those whom he or she has run over in the past and for those who carry the larger stick in the future.

A tremendous change takes place in the inner psyche and in the outer circumstances when you change your concept of mentally tough from willfulness to "willingness." In certain circles, tough means "limber, flexible, adaptable." The tough person is one who rolls with the punches, rides the waves, and moves with the tides. The tough person is one who demonstrates a willingness to cooperate, to adjust, to give up a rigid point of view for the harmony of the whole.

The will*ful* will often meet resistance, resentment, and rebellion, finding themselves in total war most of the time. The will*ing* person meets with acceptance, coordination, and even love.

The willful person will ask, "What can you do for me?" — and demands an answer.

The willing person says, "What can I do for you?" — and means it.

Fences

I once conducted a communications seminar in

Charlotte, North Carolina where an ambitious forty-year-old executive from Nashville, Tennessee, wrestled for two whole days with the ideas of vertical thinking and seeing the problem from the highest point of view. He had given up his time, he complained, not for a philosophy of the world, but for some hard-line practical facts about what to say and what to do to make his writing and speaking have more impact.

He sat in the front row, scowling at my jokes and put off "by all these abstractions." He was becoming increasingly agitated, taking out his hostility on others in the small group to which he had been assigned. By the end of the second full day, he was ready to pack it in and chalk up the whole experience on the minus side of the ledger.

But he didn't go. He went out for a jog instead. He felt he needed some exercise and some time away, to work out the tension.

As joggers know, the worst of all possible enemies are dogs. Especially in sleepy southern towns, dogs are liable to be very protective of their owners' property. As the Nashville native trotted along a back road, he heard a tremendous growl and barking that made the hair on his neck stand on end!

There, growling behind a thin wire fence about three feet high, was a huge, young, and hyper Doberman Pinscher, eyes blazing and teeth bared! The dog was about as high as the fence on all fours, and with hardly any effort at all, he could have jumped the fence. The man knew he was in trouble and stood still for a moment to see how he could get out safely.

Then, an amazing thing happened. The dog barked and barked, jumped up and down and growled, ran back and forth, but did not jump over the skimpy fence. In a flash of insight, the man realized that the dog had been conditioned to stay within the boundaries of the fence. Despite his capacity to run and jump for freedom, the dog stayed just where he was, gnashing his teeth and running back and forth in angry circles. The man jogged by, knowing he was safe from this particular doggie.

The next day, the Nashville man raised his hand. To the surprise of all in the seminar, he asked to stand before the group and say a few words. He had not volunteered for anything to this point, so everyone became quiet, not knowing what to expect.

He told his story quietly and elegantly. "In that moment,"

he reported, "I knew I was just like that dog. I can jump the fence anytime I want to. I can write, I can speak. I *can* think on many levels at the same time. No more fences for me."

The audience applauded. The man from Nashville went home free.

Comedy Is Harder

Some people carry a background thought consciously with them *all* the time. Everytime you meet them, they are thinking in their characteristic way. They *become* their background thought, no matter where they are or what they are doing.

In the 1940s, there was a lovable comic actor named Edmund Gwynne, who worked on Broadway and in films, for producer George Seton in *A Tree Grows in Brooklyn,* for example. Gwynne was a solitary, artistic sort of man who loved to talk theatre and look at life through the lens of comedy.

After performances on stage, Gwynne, with Seton and others, would often sit around in some favorite restaurant and talk about their craft. Although they disagreed on some of the fine points of acting, directing, and writing, they all seemed to agree on one thing — comedy is harder than tragedy. It is easier to make people cry than laugh. It is easier to ignite the audience to anger, fear, or hostility than to bring a smile to their faces. It is more difficult to tell a joke night after night and get a laugh than to hit an emotional note of irritation, annoyance, or desire.

Then, one day, Edmund Gwynne, great actor and comedian, disappeared. No one knew where he was or what he was doing. One day he was in town, the next day he was gone, without a trace or a warning.

For years, there was no word about Gwynne. Then, George Seton received a phone call from London. Someone had found Gwynne living alone and destitute in a coldwater flat in the middle of a particularly nasty London winter.

Seton caught the first plane and brought his long-lost friend back to Los Angeles and registered him in the old-age Actor's Home. Every day, he would go to Gwynne's bedside for an hour or so. They would talk theatre. They would argue and disagree, but they would always come back to the idea that comedy is harder — harder than anything else on stage.

Early one morning, Seton received a phone call from the home. Gwynne was dying. He had suffered a relapse and surely would be gone in a few hours. Seton jumped into his car and raced to the bedside of the dying comedian.

When he got there, Seton's heart sank. Gwynne was pale and ashen, his eyes closed, covers pulled up high under his chin. The man was very weak.

"How are you doing, Ed?" asked Seton gently.

"Not so good, George. This is it for me."

"How does it feel to die?" asked Seton. "To *really* die."

"It's tough," croaked Gwynne. "Really tough. Hard."

"Really hard, huh?"

"Yeah, but comedy's harder." And Gwynne died. Right there, with a smile on his face.

The Secret of Life

Once upon another time, when God was creating mankind in His likeness and image, there was an executive council meeting for all divisions of the enterprise. All the top angels were asked to attend, for even though everybody had deadlines to meet and budgets to prepare, God wanted their opinion on an extremely grave and pressing matter.

God was considering giving mankind the secret of life. He wanted to know where to hide this precious gift so that it would be very difficult to find and then only by the most dedicated individuals.

One angel thought that it should be sunk in the depths of the sea.

Another thought it should be buried in the bowels of the earth.

A third felt it should be encased very near the sky, at the pinnacle of the highest mountain, in the most desolate region possible.

But a fourth angel had a different point of view. "No, mankind's a tricky breed. Somebody will swim the deepest sea, dig down into the bowels of the earth, and scale the highest mountain. We should place this secret someplace where mankind would never dream of looking – right inside of himself."

God nodded in agreement, and so it was done.

How To Be A Hero

A newspaperman once pressed John F. Kennedy on his rise to the lofty status of being president of the United States. "We know you have money, good looks, power, and influence, but how did you manage to become a war hero?"

"They sank my boat," replied Kennedy.

What are your favorite stories? Look for good stories, ones that relate to the audiences you face in your everyday life. Ask your friends or professional colleagues for their stories — ones you can live by and live with. If you live with a good story for a long enough time, long enough for it to become part of your own inner life, it will become your life story.

A good story is worth a thousand textbooks or computer layouts. The lively storyteller has a finger on the pulse of the moment. The storyteller knows his or her material and is free to make an immediate contact with the audience. He or she becomes a channel and a vehicle for a common union — an open way for communication. The storyteller can touch the mind and the heart — paving the way for the other person to want to work with him or her. A good story or two can melt the ice and cool the fires of resistance.

And remember, no good story is told the same way twice. The best stories sound as if they were being told for the first time — a quality that develops naturally out of the reading aloud exercise.

Put yourself into the story. Color it with real feelings. Take the time to make it important to yourself and meaningful for those with you right now. Look for reactions in the faces and eyes of your immediate audience, and make sure your story is directed to some person in the here and now.

Stories can entertain, inform, inspire. They can get people to listen and to move — and that's the most important point of all.

9

The Formal Presentation

Here we are, at the moment of truth — the formal presentation.

Here is the time you will be going on an interview for a new position, asking your boss for a raise, meeting a client to close a sale, addressing a professional group of colleagues, or facing an emotional relative. The formal presentation is one you know is coming so you can surpass yourself and transcend your former boundaries, limitations, and fences.

The formal presentation can be a frightening and threatening affair mainly because you have time to think about it.

You have time to worry about it, time to dwell over the possibilities and potentialities for goofing it up. If you have a specific target date when you know you will have to think on your feet and say what you mean, you also have a great chance to build up the pressure on yourself. There you will be, on stage alone, with all those eyes peering in on you, waiting for you to be brilliant, devastating, unforgettable. The pressure will be on, and everyone will easily see how you react to it.

Although the formal presentation is a significant — and sometimes monumental — event, it is important to see it as part of a process, not as an event in itself. Super Bowl Sunday is the end of a whole season of preparation and elimination. A heavyweight championship follows an intensive training period designed to hone the physical and psychological strength of the fighters to a peak of excellence. The players in the finals of a tennis tournament have won all the preliminary matches.

The formal presentation brings together in one unified whole all the elements of effective communication that we have worked on to this point. You have worked on yourself, met unexpected moments with a clear, definite background thought, and have practiced the capacity to work from the inside out. Now is the time to turn on your "big guns" — your best ideas, your most positive emotions, your creative energy, your genuine enthusiasm.

Energy and *enthusiasm* — two forces that can open up new horizons for you — are the essential ingredients of a formal presentation. At the moment of delivery, nothing counts more than your ability to turn yourself on and let your inner light shine. If you want your audience to tune in and respond favorably to you, you have to tune in to yourself, possibly at a deeper level than you ever have before.

The formal presentation can mobilize your best talents and put them on display. Most of the inner work you have done with yourself is now ready to be given to the outside world. It is time for you confidently to go public.

The following ten steps are called the Creative Process Technique — C.P.T. — because they provide an objective, measurable, practical guide to bring your best inner self into a public forum. C.P.T. gives you a method to realize your goal in a logical, orderly, disciplined fashion, but it can also fire your imagination and encourage your individuality.

The ten steps of the Creative Process Technique are designed for one major purpose — to allow you to speak spontaneously and freely when facing all those eyes. Each step will focus your creative potential and build a foundation of confidence and poise so that you can meet the unknown with the assurance that you can rise to any challenge.

Once again, let us emphasize the spirit with which to approach the C.P.T. Be gentle, loving, and relaxed with yourself. Invest time in the preparation period — enough time so that you do not have to rush yourself near the finish line. When you rush yourself, you rush your talent.

All seeds need time to root and grow. All great ideas and formal presentations need time to germinate and take shape. Your *formal* presentation will take some time to *form-all*. Your first and greatest challenge is to plant early and nourish the seed day- by- day.

THE CREATIVE PROCESS TECHNIQUE

1. Who Is The Audience?

First and most important, get a clear reading on your audience. Find out about their levels of receptivity or resistance.

To whom will you be speaking?

What kind of person(s) will you be addressing?

What is their background — emotionally, financially, professionally?

What are their goals and what will they be expecting from you?

What is your relationship to these people?

Are they ready to hear what you have to say?

Since communication is a two-way street — mental and emotional — you first have to know the emotional climate of the situation to come to a deep understanding of how best to present your material.

The audience comes first. No matter how brilliant or significant your message, you must first establish a rapport. You will need to open a channel for the knowledge to flow through. Your words need first to be received before they can be used.

As much as possible, visualize your audience. Try to *see* them as they will be. Clarify your mental, visual picture of who they are, where they are, and where they might be going. If you do not know exactly whom you will be addressing, make some calls. Ask some questions. Play detective.

In order to warm them up, don't go in cold. Get a feel for those people in front of you because if they begin to turn against you, your message will go out the window.

Many presenters make a cardinal mistake in thinking too much about what they want and not enough about their audience. They concentrate so intently on their personal goals that they really forget about the true targets — the heart and mind of the audience.

The key question in step one of the C.P.T. is "What can I give to this audience to help them do their work better and enjoy their lives more?"

Think *give*. Let your material be offered with the feeling of a give. *Never tell your audience what to think or what they "must" do*. Simply offer an idea with your own energy and enthusiasm and suggest a way to embody that idea.If you make an offering, the audience will not feel forced or intimidated. They will want to reach out for you because of your attitude and aptitude for communicating at the moment. Know the needs, fears, and desires of your audience. That will provide the best and most trustworthy clue to your own approach to your material.

If at any step along the Creative Process, you feel lost, confused, not quite sure of what to do next, return to this beginning. Ask yourself: who is my audience? What can I give to them? What can I say to make them feel better about themselves?

What can I do for you? This should be your first question.

2. What Is My Task?

As suggested earlier, there are two components of the idea of task — the business task and the personal task. The business task is what you want people to do with you in the marketplace. The personal task is what you are doing in yourself to bring about the desired business.

What effect do I want to have on this audience?

What do I want these persons to do, think, or feel when I finish speaking?

What relationship do I want to establish?

What one thing do I want them to remember most?

What visual picture do I want them to have of me?

For example, your business task might be to make a sale and write an order. But since you know that this particular customer is busy and often irritable, your personal task might be to *relax under the pressure*. Since you might well expect objections and a testy attitude, you need to prepare your own inner flexibility and poise even at this early stage.

In many cases, your conscious personal task — your active, positive, progressive background thought — could very well be *the way* to make the sale and write the order. The way in which you handle yourself under pressure could be just the element that makes this person want to buy from you. How many times have you found yourself selling yourself as well as the product?

Having clarified your visual audience, *write down* your business task and your personal task. Choose a background thought that is right for *this particular person*. In the days before the actual presentation, practice this particular background thought during your business rounds. In other words, warm up your background thought system before you actually climb on the stage where you will give your performance. The presentation might be made on an actual stage, in an office, or in a conference room. Wherever it is, nothing is more important than the execution of your background thought.

Clarify your task in all its dimensions. Commit your goal to paper and review it often. It will be easy to get caught up in the nuts and bolts later; therefore, it is very important to imprint your goal on your own inner psyche.

Once you define your task, see it as already being done. Get the feeling that you have already accomplished the desired result. At least in your own mind, let there be no doubt that everything will go as you have pictured it. Cultivate the feeling of winning by working with these positive pictures of achieving yor goal. This will lead to a genuine winning attitude, free of concern, worry, or hurry.

Step two of the C.P.T. builds a genuine sense of purpose from within. You won't have to fake enthusiasm or manufacture energy if you believe that your task can be accomplished, if you can see it as already done. With that *feeling* of success, you will be free to improvise and have a good time at the moment of presentation.

3. Plug In The P.R.E.P.

At this stage of the Creative Process, you begin to actively deal with your material. Here, you collect your data, conduct your research, gather the evidence from which you will determine your major point of view.

Gathering your data is one thing, but *interpreting* it is something else again. For a great presentation, you must do more than *report* your research. Interpret it. Give it form. Cut away the excess and get to the essence.

Many people have found it helpful to make a special P.R.E.P. folder. Whenever they find an article or have a flash of insight or come across some important piece of evidence, they write it on an index card and drop it into the folder without regard to order or form. After a few days or several weeks of data collecting, they spread out all the evidence in front of them — then they begin to arrange it in the P.R.E.P. Formula.

When looking over your data, be sure to maintain an overview. In a psychological sense, stand above your material and see how it can be used to relate to your particular visual audience and to realize your goal. From the evidence in front of you, evidence that *has been* gathered from past events, what *could be*? In front of you, there is a message concerning the probabilities of things to come, but what are the possibilities? You have the story of the past staring you in the face, but what do you want to build in the future? What can be made of this evidence to surpass the limitations of the past?

This *could be* line of thinking very often will kick off the most progressive point of view possible. The *could be* perspective leads to a special kind of interpretation. By seeing the facts of the matter from the highest point of view, you help yourself become part of the solution instead of being part of the problem.

Keeping the audience in mind in this step will help you select your material in a suitable manner. The audience will help you to determine what is appropriate and what is not. You do not have to give expression to all your data — only the segment that is right for *this* audience.

Remember that the P.R.E.P. is a thinking process, but also a format to give the actual presentation. Think out your material in the P.R.E.P. before you get on stage; it also may be the form you speak in. Once this format is firmly in mind, it is very much like a game plan. If something happens that is distracting during the actual presentation, simply refer back to your mental P.R.E.P. Where are you in the formula? That will put you on track and enable you to overcome the distraction or detour.

Remember that the final element of the P.R.E.P Formula includes the *action* you want the audience to consider. Be sure you have a clear picture of what to do with your material. Tie the date to a specific recommendation — at least in your own mind.

4. Write An Outline; Talk Into A Tape Recorder

Having gathered and edited your data into the P.R.E.P. form, write an outline and practice talking it through into a tape recorder. In the privacy of your office or home, sit down with a page outline and talk it out. *Improvise.* Simply practice the sense of talking to the person you have selected as your visual audience.

If you do not know who your audience is precisely, practice the sense of talking to a friend or colleague in business. This exercise is designed to promote the feeling that you are talking to an actual person, someone real, rather than an *abstract audience.*

The tone of this tape session should be casual and informal. What would you say to this person if he or she were sitting in the room with you? Don't visualize yourself in the formal situation in the location where you will actually be speaking. Just get the sense of talking one-to-one, with no big deal at stake. You are simply running through your presentation to get some comments from this friend, much as if you are in rehearsal and polishing your act. You are not *performing* now. You are just talking to someone as if he or she were going to help you clarify your own manner and style of speaking.

After you talk to the tape recorder as if a friend were present, listen to yourself. Listen to your words as if you were the other person. How do you sound to you — especially in the sense of being honest and believable?

> *Does this person sound like he (or she) is really talking to me — or is he (or she) concentrating on content?*
>
> *Is this person talking to me or at me?*

Is this person giving something of him (or her) self, or just reciting words?

This is where the reading aloud exercise really comes into play. If you exercise in a regular way by reading aloud material that does not particularly apply to your work, you build up your quality of believability. If you can take new and strange material and make that come alive, you certainly will add quality and dimension to material you already know something about.

Be gentle with yourself when listening to yourself, but also be objective. Let spontaneous phrases come to you each time. Don't try to say exactly the same words as you did the night before. Jot down some phrases or code words that you particularly like, but don't make anything rigid or definite.

Never write a word-for-word script for yourself. Always give yourself the freedom to improvise and find the right word at the moment. As if by magic, you will find something coming to you at the moment of the actual presentation if you let yourself alone and free yourself to be spontaneous.

5. How Could This Be Better?

After listening to yourself talking out your presentation in an informal way, look for how you can make this better. Very often, *better* means *shorter*. What can you cut out? What can you edit?

When sitting back and listening to yourself as critic, what is in this talk that makes it special? What makes you special? What quality that you know you have sets you apart from everybody else? Your warmth, your sensitivity, your sense of humor? Have your own personal, individual qualities come out on the tape? Do you sound like yourself as you could be or do you sound as you think you *should* sound in front of this audience?

In other words, take some time to put yourself more into your words. The words will always give the information, but what you add to your words will leave the overall impression.

Look to express yourself. Let your intuitive voice move in you and through you. You can rise to any occasion by inviting that imaginative dimension within you to come to the surface. With your "partner" present in you, you can fill in the moment with your feeling — and always be on target.

6. Put Your Material To Sleep

Putting your material "to sleep" means not overworking your presentation practice. You don't have to go over and over it because it can very easily become stale and routine.

There is a very delicate balance that can be maintained if you just forget about your material after you practice the first five steps of the C.P.T. By regular and consistent practice of the other exercises in this book, you have been opening up a channel into your subconscious and superconscious levels. These dimensions of your mind respond best to suggestions and calm and gentle direction. The less you agonize and worry about how you will do at the moment of delivery, the better the delivery will be.

By putting your material to sleep, you allow the creative unconscious mind to do the work. In that realm, the imagination, intuition, and inspirational forces are at play, which far surpass anything the intellect could conjure up. When you let your material sleep by taking your mind off it, you let it root and become part of your emotional bloodstream.

You don't have to stand over a seed to make the roots grow. You simply have to give it a little water and weed the soil. Then you let the natural forces do the work. If you start to doubt the ability of the seed to take root, you might pull it out just to make sure everything is happening the way it should. All you do then is impede the process and perhaps kill the seed.

After you practice for your designated time during the day, let go all concern and conscious thought about your formal presentation. Especially if this presentation is very important, take time away from it. You will only strangle your own spontaneity with worry and tension, so you can best cooperate with the creative process by dissolving your concern.

Trust your intuition and hunches. That plane of yourself is ready, willing, and able to direct you to the right words while the chips are down, the heat is on, and the money is on the table.

You rarely have to make things happen. You always have to let things happen. Say what you are listening to. Be a messenger, not an "expert."

7. Packaging Counts

No matter how good your product or important your message, people see and respond to the package it is wrapped in. In our society, packaging counts, perhaps more than it should. Nevertheless, how you wrap your package gives a tangible indication of how you feel about yourself.

By packaging, we mean several things. First and foremost is your dress and grooming. Over the years, I have been impressed by the visual impact that clean, pressed, expensive clothes can make on an audience. One prominent doctor reported attending a conference. When the speaker came to the podium, he wore a tailored, up-to-date, stylish suit. The doctor said, "Just by the way he looked, I was ready to listen to anything he had to say."

Although budgets may be tight, strongly consider investing in a suit, or an appropriate outfit, that may be more than you usually spend. If you buy a suit of clothes that is $100 or $200 more than you think you can really afford, you will have a special feeling when you wear it. If you see this expenditure as a symbol of the prosperity you could enjoy, you will project a picture and feeling of success. If your content lives halfway up to your image, you will open channels of further communication.

This does not mean that packaging is most important. Some elegant, tailored, manicured people have empty heads and tortured souls, but the combination of well thought out material and good grooming is a fine way of objectifying your spirit.

The feelings of the audience are definitely affected by what they see, so experiment with your clothing and colors to find the look that is right for you. If you look good, you will feel good. If you feel good, you will be good.

You might also try to go into your formal presentation with a couple of crisp, new bills in your pocket, just to get the feel of "having enough." It really doesn't matter what denomination of bill you carry. What is important is the feeling that you have money already in your pocket that is real and available to you right now. It is mainly a symbol of what is to come if you practice the principles. Carrying extra cash is a physical reminder of your spiritual bank account. With the feeling that you have enough right now to meet any emergency that might come about, you can be free to move and speak with an attitude of freedom. In this frame of mind, you don't have to *make the sale.*

All you have to do is express yourself to your fullest potential. If you have been given the opportunity to make the presentation, it simply means that you have the opportunity to build a bridge and create a positive relationship by being relaxed, in tune, and on top of the potential pressure, you can pay better attention to your audience and serve their needs. By getting yourself in tune from the inside, you have a foundation for your actions and your reactions. You have presence of mind.

It is also a good idea to leave something behind in writing. You will make a definite impression by your speaking style, but leave the door open for people to contact you in a specific way. Leave a card, a brochure, a folder that people can look at and *see you.*

This verbal-written presentation combination is tough to beat.You may not get every role or close every sale, but you will not be beating yourself. Any one audience may have no need for your particular kind of service, but that only means that this is not where you are supposed to be for your own growth.

Don't burn any bridges behind you. Package yourself as you would like to see yourself. This is a good chance to fashion your *could be* self.

Packaging counts. What you invest in your outside package can very well determine your returns. Know your audience, but always go for your best.

8. Energy And Enthusiasm

You have made your preparation and you have wrapped your package attractively and appropriately. The day has come when you are in front of your designated audience. Now what? What is more important while you are actually standing on that stage or sitting in that office?

Energy and enthusiasm. Nothing is more infectious than enthusiasm or more attractive than lively energy.

Energy and enthusiasm always communicate that intangible "something more" to you. Without energy and enthusiasm, the presentation will always seem to be missing something. It is important to understand that the level of energy required in the formal presentation is different and higher than the level you use when driving to work, watching television, or strolling in the country.

The energy needed for speaking is like a higher gear that you can easily shift into when you are relaxed, receptive, and open to the opportunity for service that is present when you speak to this audience. In fact, the sense of drama and importance of the moment will often push your adrenalin button. You will be flooded with a tremendous sense of excitement and genuine feeling just by leaving yourself alone and relaxing your body.

Enthusiasm is a function of your relationship with your material — your personal feelings about what you are saying. You have to care about your material. You have to make it your own. Most importantly, you will need to make what you say important to yourself.

In modern-day corporations, many people feel alienated from their material. They look to the facts and the statistics of the matter to turn them on or turn them off. Because many individuals in many professions work at their jobs without any sense of being personally involved, nothing really excites them. They put in their time and pick up their checks.

But the material can never really turn you on. *You* turn *yourself* on to the material or you turn yourself off. The material is outside of you and has no power over you — or it shouldn't. You make the choice of what happens in you, so don't make the mistake of having your level of enthusiasm depend on your material.

The truth is that nothing is more important than your personal growth. This material and this opportunity to deliver this presentation have been given to you to make something out of them. If you have taken the preliminary steps and have taken the time to prepare mentally, you will have "courted" your material and made it your own.

But if you have resisted investing time in the proper preparation, you will be wrestling with the material at the moment of delivery. Consciously or unconsciously, you will transmit your basic attitude and feeling to the audience, so it is important to dissolve any feelings of resistance you might be carrying about your content.

All content must be made personal. Everything you say needs to be important to you. If you see the presentation in the larger circle of providing you with the opportunity to master your speaking style, every presentation is important to your evolution as a human being. Each presentation is more than a factual set of data presented for a business purpose. Every presentation is a reflection of your inner state of mind.

Within you is the cause of what happens to you. If for nothing else, be enthusiastic about facing all those eyes because something inside of you has contributed to your being there. Being there is a sign that you are able to grow, to care, to share the creative dimension in yourself.

Make your material more important to yourself, not because your company deserves it or your boss demands it. Make your material more important because *you* deserve it. You cannot water down your enthusiasm without watering down your talent.

Turn yourself on. Let your light shine. Go for the best within yourself. You determine your own level of involvement. You take command of your ship. That is the difference between slavery and freedom.

9. Record And Review

You are your own best teacher, or you could be.

After each formal presentation you make or important meeting you attend, take a few minutes with your journal and write a review of your own performance. Perhaps you could call these short entries about what happened in you, for you, or to you the "Message of the Meeting."

What is the *message* in the encounter? What could you use for the next time? What went right and what went wrong? Did you execute your intention? Did you act upon your game plan? To what degree? What happened unexpectedly? Did you relax under pressure and think on your feet?

In other words, evaluate yourself. Be your own best critic. Look for your successes, but also look for areas of improvement.

Then, in preparation for your next formal situation, read over the messages from the past. Look back and see what you want to work for this time. See what ideas, tasks, or background thoughts worked for you, and what ones didn't. By writing a short report on yourself, you have a record to help you in the future.

In a short time, you will see patterns begin to emerge. Certain efforts you made had positive results — people responded the way you intended. Sometimes you did not achieve the desired response, even when you feel you did a super job. From the perspective of time, look back. It is easier to get an objective overview after a little time passes, so it is very important to invest a few minutes for a talk with yourself after a major presentation.

It is just a matter of keeping tabs on yourself. Nobody else can really do it for you. Most people are too busy in what they want, need, or desire to keep a book on you. Like everything else, the "record and review section" of the Creative Process Technique is something you have to do for yourself to give you the slight edge.

There will be much you can learn from this kind of recording and reviewing — lessons that can translate into confidence, assurance, and poise under pressure.

10. Enjoy The Process

Any struggle you may have with expressing yourself is essentially a struggle with yourself. It is not your boss, your job, your level of formal education, or your mistake-ridden past that is holding you back and bringing you down. The seed of discontent is always an inside job, and the remedy is to weed your own psychic garden day-by-day.

There are many poets, philosophers, and psychologists who claim that joy is the natural state of the human being. Organically and inherently, each of us has the capacity to enjoy, to love, to be thankful for being where we are and who we are. But just like intelligence or creativity, joy needs to be claimed and proclaimed, or else it tends to wither and shrivel up.

That is why it is so crucial for you to wrap this entire creative process with a ribbon of joy. Just as being resentful is a choice that you make, so too is being joyful. You can enjoy yourself by taking control of your own thoughts, feelings, and desires, or you can be resentful by allowing others to be the strongest influence in your life.

Set *joy* as a goal for yourself and relax into that state. As you practice the exercises and internalize the ideas of this book, you will find a tremendous sense of joy and release in expressing yourself in the very same situations in which you held yourself back before.

There always comes a moment in the course of this study when you find yourself thinking on many levels at the same time. Something will come to you — a person, a situation, an unexpected meeting — that will be the perfect setting for you to practice vertical thinking and relaxing under pressure.

At a certain bend in the road, you will have the feeling of being totally in control and in touch with the natural flow of energy in the universe. Invariably, hundreds and thousands of people who have practiced these principles find themselves in the flow of a magnificent, generous, loving presence, which then guides, shapes, and supports their every action.

When Emerson said that around every circle, a larger circle may be drawn, he meant that you can expand your life by allowing your inner spirit to surface. You can transcend any past mistakes by learning from them. You can overcome any past habits by rising above them. You can speak without fear by steering into it. You can think on your feet and say what you mean because that is what you are supposed to do.

Anything less is frustration and limitation. Anything less than love and joy in the creative process keeps you back from the good that is yours to claim.

Every person is creative. You create the quality of your life by the quality of your thoughts. You create the reality of your speaking skills by your conscious and unconscious choices.

It is not easy to let go of the past. It is not easy to surpass yourself. It is not easy to transcend the circle you have set for yourself and expand into a larger circle. It is not easy, but it is possible.

When you can think quickly and decisively and have good stories to tell, there is more than money on the table. There is richness of soul. There is abundance of spirit. There is meaning in the day-to-day routine of living. As a matter of fact, when you get into the express business, you will not get tied up in the busy-ness of making a living. Each day in the express business is an adventure and a challenge, an opportunity to open the way for your imprisoned splendor to escape.

When you practice these principles, they will always work for you and with you to help you draw larger and larger circles around your former set of experiences. You can confidently expect your financial status, your standard of living, and your number of positive relationships to grow when you think on your feet with presence of mind.

By polishing your speaking and thinking skills, you will be polishing your inner self.

One day, the great artist Michelangelo was walking down the streets of Florence. He spied a huge slab of marble that another sculptor had botched and was about to throw away.

"There's an angel in that slab of stone," Michelangelo said to himself. He purchased the very same block, which the other sculptor thought to be worthless.

Michelangelo began to sculpt that block of stone. He began to whittle and polish, always seeing "the angel" in his mind's eye. Never losing the vision, he worked with the sense of a mission — with the desire to pare off the excess and free the essence that was "imprisoned" inside. He loved that stone and the angel within it. Working day after day, step after step, stage after stage, one day he "gave birth."

When he was finished, the world had the statue of *David*.

I encourage you to *go for it* — go for the perfect person yourself. Visualize the perfect angel inside and sculpt yourself into that image.

Pay the price and win the game. Stake your claim. There is nothing to it but to do it.

The role of the good advisor is to make him- or herself ever more expendable. At some point, the "teacher" bids the "student" farewell. These chapters have been presented so that you can be more productive and efficient in your personal and professional life. What I am describing here is not fantasy and imagination, but fact and imagination. After many years of experience, I am certain that each of us has an incredible potential for excellence built into the psychic system.

We are wired for prosperity, abundance, and successful living, but we must turn on our own lights. Another word for light is *idea*. We must choose the thoughts that make us happy, free, willing to express. Nobody can do that for us, although we often let other people choose our thoughts and beliefs. We must work on ourselves to really do our own job.

To help you keep in mind the principle of this book, keep in mind these ten commandments of creative communications:

1. Understand your role.
2. Visualize your goal.
3. Prepare a game plan.
4. Feel that you *can*.
5. Look for the good.

6. Go for the *could*.
7. Let go of the past.
8. Don't try to climb fast.
9. Nurture your dream.
10. Create a good team; tune in the beam!

10

Thoughts For the Road

The most important teachers in my life have always left me with news I could use. The most influential persons in my past have given me a phrase, a sentence, a motto that I could remember and practice when the heat was on. In turn, I offer you a few thoughts for the road, some concise phrases to keep conscious when circumstances seem to be going against you.

Around every circle, a larger circle may be drawn.

More important than what is happening to me or around me is what is happening in me.

142

I always have a choice — a choice about how I prefer to react to what is happening out there.

Nothing is more important than my background thought for today.

Relaxation is the key to the vault of riches.

When I rush myself, I rush my talent.

What effect do I want to have on my audience?

I will not let the limitations of others be my criteria for behavior.

Think from the twenty-eighth floor.

Comedy is harder.

Within me is the cause for what happens to me.

Relax my shoulders.

I am a living magnet.

To be prosperous, I will act as if I have money in the bank already.

It takes twenty-one days of calm, patience, and warmth for an egg to hatch.

When I am ready, I will attain what I am destined to attain.

If I am not a part of the solution, I am part of the problem.

For more information about the *Think on Your Feet* seminars, write to:

Think on Your Feet
152 W. 58th St.
Suite 9D
New York, NY 10019